PURPOSE OVER PERFECTION

Praise for

PURPOSE OVER PERFECTION

I've often hidden behind perfectionism without fully understanding why. This book gently uncovers what's beneath trying to be perfect and offers something even greater... freedom! You'll laugh, you may cry, but most of all, you'll feel seen. For anyone exhausted from trying to hold it all together, this book is a deep breath of fresh air!

AMANDA HAYHURST
AUTHOR, SPEAKER, BIBLE TEACHER,
AND BESTSELLING AUTHOR OF **PRAY FOR HIM**

EMBRACING GOD'S CALLING
IN THE MIDDLE OF THE CHAOS

Purpose

OVER

Perfection

ANDI HARPER
host of "For The Love Of Chaos" podcast

DEDICATION

To my beautiful children—This is for you.

You make me dream bigger, laugh harder, and love deeper than I could ever imagine. Your faces are my inspiration in every single thing that I do. You all are the steady reminders of what matters most in life.

Being your momma is my greatest calling and my most favorite adventure. I hope you always put God first in everything and that no dreams are ever too small!

I hope you always chase after them, just as I have my own dreams within every page of this book. You each remind me daily that purpose isn't found in perfection, but in faithfulness.

I love you to the ends of the earth.

EASTER 2023- WHEN EVERYONE WAS DRESSED CUTE, AND NONE OF THE BABIES HAD ON DIRTY DINOSAUR PAJAMAS.

TABLE OF CONTENTS

The Myth of Having It Together

Growing up, we were always told to dream big and set big goals, and I definitely did—just in my own frazzled way. Dreams, ideas, business plans? I have a whole collection. You could say I'm a jack-of-all trades but a master of none. Over the years, I have been a cosmetologist, photographer, spray tan artist, blogger, boutique owner, and podcaster. But not every dream in our hearts is a part of the divine plan that God has in store for us.

Last year, I bought a super cute pink tent and soft-launched a snow cone business. My six children (yes, six) ate most of the profit (literally). So, it was fun while it lasted, but that idea melted in the summer heat.

I even had a cool idea to start writing obituaries. It sounds morbid, I know. Don't worry, I never followed through on that one. But if you ever need one that holds character and a little jazz, hit me up and I'll see what I can do.

One dream that you can be thankful that I didn't achieve is the goal of singing. Your girl can't carry a tune in a bucket. We can all be thankful that dream was squashed early on. The Bible says to sing a joyful noise to the Lord, and honey, there ain't a thing joyful about my singing abilities. But here's the thing: my creativity in my crazy dreams was never lacking.

My follow-through sometimes was. And I've learned something along the way—not every dream is a God thing.

But this book is. I can tell you that confidently, without any doubt or hesitation. And even when I drag my feet, God always finishes what He starts.

I've always struggled with focus. Growing up in the '90s, terms like ADD were only used in math problems. It wasn't really "a thing" people talked about. But if there was such a thing as a struggle bus, your girl was definitely driving it. (There is a sticker on my van today that says "The Struggle Bus.") I recognize that flaw and own it wholeheartedly. But this book is a testament of how God uses our flaws for good.

My brain may be scattered, and my ducks are definitely not in a perfectly lined row—I may have even lost a couple along the way, but I eventually gathered them all up.

But the point is this: I am the poster person for imperfection. But God saw fit to use me anyway. In spite of myself. In spite of all my flaws and imperfections.

That dream He placed on your heart?

That heavy burden that keeps you up at night?

That thing that may seem out of reach?

It's not out of reach for Him. Nothing is too heavy or big for Him.

Let this book be a perfect, or rather a perfectly imperfect, example of that.

I would like to think of this book as my past twenty years of life experience all tied up in a bow, but that bow unraveled and looks far more like duct tape (or on good days, the cute, patterned washi tape). Being a mom to six kiddos comes with a whole lot of chaos and seasons of survival. For many years, I have beaten myself up over every little thing. I've constantly battled never feeling quite good enough. This is an epidemic in motherhood, and you won't convince me otherwise. I partially blame social media. Ok, more than partially; I feel like it takes a lot of the blame.

So many platforms give a picture-perfect account of womanhood, as well as motherhood. Neatly organized homes, aesthetic wardrobes, and hobbies that seem to come so naturally. Influencers' posts romanticize things like gardening and sourdough and make them look easy. I'm not knocking these influencers—I genuinely admire them. I just know that what comes easy to some may not come as easily to others . . . and I am those others. I tried my hand at both and neither worked out in my favor. Goats ate my tomatoes, and I accidentally killed my beautiful, bubbly sourdough.

Now. Before you dive in, let me just say: this is *not* the book that's going to teach you steps to finally get your life together. Let me put things into perspective for you: as I am writing this, I am sipping my cold coffee and being silently judged by a mountain of unmatched socks. Along with the laundry, there are random trails of Legos like sourdough breadcrumbs through my house and there's a random Christmas tree on my fireplace.

I should also mention it is June.

I put this book off for years because I was waiting to "get my life together a little more." Then I turned thirty-six and realized life doesn't slow down as we age—it only speeds up. And my knees aren't what they used to be when I try to catch up. Even though thirty-six may not seem like a significant milestone, with that birthday came a lot of wisdom, healing, and revelation. And I finally realized: I will never reach that imaginary level of "having it all together." It's simply not in the cards for me. My cards are bent, scattered, tattered, and have slight coffee stains. But they can still be played just fine.

I had an amazing counselor once tell me that I dealt with my cards in a beautiful way. Certain sessions seemed rather dysfunctional—tears fell as I talked through the most broken season of my life, but in the next breath, I would spin it into something humorous, and we would nearly fall onto the floor laughing. This book will be a lot like those sessions—some tears, but also a lot of laughs.

I've spent too many years beating myself up over every little thing. I fought a constant battle of never feeling quite good enough in any capacity. I've had many seasons of barely hanging on, seasons where I held on for dear life by the unraveling hem of Jesus' garment, but He *always* got me through.

And here is something I have come to discover along my journey, God does not call us to be perfect. Ever. In fact, most of Jesus' disciples and the people He walked closest with were heavily flawed and full of imperfections themselves. Why? Because only people who admit their brokenness and imperfections realize their need for a Savior.

And though none of us are perfect, God created each of us with a *purpose.* Jesus doesn't mind if we show up in our messy buns, with our cold coffee, or with spit up on our T-shirts. He just wants to meet us where we are, right in the middle of our messes.

Here is the thing I want you to know before you dive in: *Joy and sorrow can coexist. Laughter can accompany grief. Peace can shake hands with chaos. Some of life's greatest moments and chapters in our lives entangle all of these emotions. Sometimes the world tries to make us choose one or the other—joy or sorrow, laughter or tears, brokenness or strength. These emotions are not a contradiction to one another; they are evidence of the goodness of God. And when we look to Jesus, truth will inform all of those emotions.*

So come along, friend.

Come as you are—messy bun, cold coffee, and yesterday's makeup. If you're carrying a heavy heart and a messy house, if you're smiling on the outside but barely holding it together, you're in good company here. Be ready to laugh, and maybe even cry. And together we will embrace the chaos and conquer the messes. Hand in hand, we will discover what life looks like when we ditch perfection and start pursuing God's purpose in our motherhood, marriage, and everyday lives.

PART 1

God Calls You Before You Get It Together

God never asked us

TO BE FLAWLESS,

he asked us

TO BE FAITHFUL.

The Perfection Trap

A crooked little grin spilled across the chubby cheeks of my youngest son as I rushed to get him out of his car seat. It was as if his nine-month-old self already knew the mistake we'd made that morning, and he couldn't contain his joy. I was in utter shock and disbelief when we all arrived at church in our Sunday best, and my sweet, grinning, chunky boy was still in his dirty dinosaur pajamas that he had slept in the night before.

You see, it wasn't just any Sunday.

It was Easter.

There are a couple of times a year that I attempt to coordinate outfits for my family. It's not something that happens very often. It's a selfish pursuit that is more for me, because I can "oooo" and "ahhh" about how cute they all are in their matching attire. This particular Easter happened to also be the first Easter for our second set of twins, Cub and Cozi. It was also the spring that we had five children, ages five and under. Weeks before, I had ordered adorable, matching outfits for all five of our children. Complete with bows, suspenders, and even fedoras. I could hardly contain the giddiness bubbling in my momma heart about seeing them all matching for church.

Anyone who has children is well aware that Sunday mornings are far from easy. It seemed like no matter how hard I tried to prepare diaper bags, wardrobes, and breakfast plans the night before, things didn't quite flow that morning as easily as I'd hoped. At this point in my life, I was also nursing the twins and running on very little sleep, all while battling postpartum depression. Our sweet two-year-old Dax was also going through a long-winded streaking phase that he had picked up during potty training. Each time we got him dressed, he would peel his clothes off faster than I could peel the banana he was having for breakfast. During this time, he also developed a rather unhealthy toddler obsession with pacifiers, and he had two or three dangling from his mouth and in his hands at all times.

It was the best of times, and it was the worst of times.

I was in a form of survival mode that I'd never quite been in before. Survival mode with a chronic case of leaking and cracked nipples. Nevertheless, as I attempted to hide the dark circles under my eyes that morning and threw on my own Easter dress, that was snug from a little baby weight that stayed a little longer than I would have liked, I could hardly wait to see my babies dressed in their outfits. You see, I longed for the perfect family picture. It was something that hadn't happened just yet without a baby crying, a tantrum, or some fighting from my oldest twins.

As a photographer, I made a living from getting the perfect picture for other families. That was something I had become really good at. No matter the ages of their children, no matter the phase they were in, I could meet them there and somehow manage to capture giggles and smiles. But when it came to my own family, it wasn't so easy. I really, *really* wanted a good picture as a family of seven that Easter.

My husband Cody and I have always been pretty good at tag-teaming. Although he wasn't always the best at getting up during the nighttime hours, he was always incredibly helpful during the day. Just like many Sunday mornings, we hurriedly dressed all five of the babies while rushing to get out the door. Over the sounds of *Mickey Mouse Clubhouse* blaring, giggling, and footsteps running throughout the house, we tried to communicate the best that we could, but it was hard to hear one another due to the chaos happening in every corner of our home. But that morning, I tried a little extra hard. Our sweet little Cub, our youngest twin son, had issues with spitting up. Because of that, we always delayed dressing him during feeding. We had learned that the hard way many times before. Sometime throughout that morning, there was a crossed line in communication between my husband and me. I wonder, often, who in their right mind ever wrote that song that says, "Easy Like Sunday Morning." Apparently, they didn't have children. And they most definitely didn't have five of them.

I felt so accomplished as we ran out the door to barely make it on time to get a seat for church. Once we arrived at church, I swiftly swung open the car door and realized my plans, most definitely, suddenly had a wrench thrown into them. You see, I thought Cody had grabbed the outfit to put in the bag, and Cody thought I had gotten it. Everyone was perfectly dressed in their cute little outfits, except for one.

I look back now on that story and laugh so hard. But in the moment, it wasn't funny at all, and it even brought out some tears from me. Granted, I know that was something very minor to cry about. But throw in the hormones from breastfeeding, the daunting feeling like I never got anything right, and it was a recipe for a disastrous, highly emotional meltdown. In my mind, I had imagined this would be the one morning where I could feel like I *somewhat* had my life together. Even if it was just for one morning. One picture.

Those plans came unraveling at the sight of those dirty dinosaur pajamas. This morning came at a time in my life when I worried a lot more about opinions that never mattered. As I've gotten older, I have learned to release the weight of others' opinions to God. But, before I did, I wasted so much energy worrying about what other people might think. I also didn't "roll with the punches" as well then as I do now. I would find myself flailing in the murky waters of disappointment like a child throwing a temper tantrum.

Something about motherhood magnifies the desire to "get everything right." Especially in those early years of motherhood. And in those many, many moments when things don't go as planned, we can feel crushed under the weight of guilt and disappointment.

Chasing After the Wind

If you were to ask any given woman whether she was trying to be perfect in her own life, more than likely, the answer would be "no." Perfection doesn't typically walk into motherhood wearing a name tag that says, "Hello, my name is Perfection, but my nickname is Unrealistic Expectations."

It shows up dressed like "normal."

Like "being put-together."

We swipe on mascara and put on uncomfortable Spanx to make ourselves feel a bit better.

Seeking perfection looks like pressure. Pressure to keep a perfectly cleaned house, with a home-cooked meal on the table each night, all while keeping your sanity and drinking enough water each day.

It looks like comparison. It's in the car line at school, you look at the moms passing you by driving newer, trendier SUVs, while you're still driving your trusty minivan with dings and scratches all up the side.

It looks like constant self-criticism. No one judges us as hard as we judge ourselves. This begins the moment your feet hit the floor each morning. You glance in the mirror and instantly begin the judging, *the harsh judging*. You see dark circles, the extra pounds, and the grey strands that need more maintenance.

Seeking perfection looks like "I just want to get it all right." It tries to convince us that if we can control enough pieces, enough outfits, enough schedules, enough behavior, enough housework, then we can finally relax.

But that rest never comes. I am convinced that if I stayed up twenty hours working endlessly on tasks and chores around our home, I would still never be caught up. So many times, I have described my efforts as being like a hamster on a wheel. Running, chasing, never slowing down, yet I feel like I've gotten nowhere. Someone once told me that trying to keep a clean house with kids is like brushing your teeth while eating Oreos. How true and fitting.

But the thing about this perfection trap is this—it's sneaky. It isn't loud. But it's always there, even if it's in the back of our minds. It's a losing battle. Perfection doesn't bring us peace in any capacity; instead, it brings pressure. Pressure to do and be all the things that we were never meant to be. Our human instincts feed us the lie that perfection is possible. So we chase after it. Hard. But instead of finding it, we end up exhausted and epically disappointed, because perfection doesn't exist, sister. It's just a trap.

In Ecclesiastes 2:11, Solomon puts into words this exact feeling, "But as I looked at everything I had worked so hard to accomplish, it was all meaningless, like chasing the wind. There was nothing really worthwhile anywhere." Solomon, known for his wisdom, had been on an endless quest to find meaning and satisfaction through every imaginable earthly route possible. Through lavish gardens, houses, vineyards, massive herds of livestock, gold, silver, and wealth.

He would be considered highly successful by most. He seemingly had it "all together." Just like the mom with the brand-spanking new SUV. And none of those things are bad things. Yet, when he reflected on all his labor and accomplishments and his seemingly "perfect life," he realized and proclaimed through God's Word that it was all meaningless.

That's the thing about "chasing the wind;" you can never grasp it in your hands. Temporal things and our best efforts will only leave our souls dry and our bodies and minds exhausted. We were meant for more.

Embracing Imperfection

Not to sound arrogant, because you know that's not me, but *embracing imperfection* is *kinda* my expertise. I may not be able to tell you how to get it all together. But I can help you find peace when you don't. I no longer chase perfectionism.

It hasn't always been that way, though. Hence my panic on that Easter Sunday morning. I've come a long way. I've learned that in order to embrace imperfection, we must embrace honesty first.

We have to be honest with ourselves. Hard I know. Especially on days like today as I write from a slight state of exhaustion. I want to tell myself that I still have another couple days of spraying dry shampoo on my unwashed hair, but I know that's a lie. Embracing honesty isn't an easy task. It can feel a bit like giving an awkward hug to a distant relative at a once-a-year family reunion. But do it anyway.

I had to begin to ask myself some hard questions:

- What am I trying to prove?
- Does this scenario really matter?
- Am I looking for acceptance or approval from people or from God?

Embracing imperfection for me has looked like coming to terms with my messy bun and my messy house. There is a sign that hangs crooked in my home, how fitting, that says, "Bless This Mess." I love it. Because it describes me, my home, and my life in the best way. That's what embracing imperfection means. Let the picture be a little crooked, because I know as soon as I fix it, my little girl will bump her scooter on the wall while riding by and knock it crooked again. Yes, I let them ride scooters in the house. I know. I'm that mom that probably needs a little more rules and a lot more structure, but I already told you, this isn't that kind of book, remember?

Embracing imperfection means being honest with your kids too. I never ever want my kids to grow up and think that their mom had it all figured out. If I'm being transparent, and girl, you know I am, they will all grow up and know beyond a shadow of a doubt what a mess that I truly was. And I say that laughing, I'm giggling as I read that statement out loud.

But they love me anyways.

Embracing imperfection looks like apologizing on the days you get it wrong. Maybe when you get overstimulated and raise your voice at your kids. Or when you give your husband the silent treatment two days in a row because he failed to help you with the house. Our imperfections don't disqualify us; they make up who we are. As women, as moms, as wives, we wear a lot of hats. To our families we are cooks, chauffeurs, managers, teachers, nurses, referees, housekeepers, cheerleaders, and therapists. But we aren't God. We're just women. Women who get tired. Women who forget things. Women who forget to turn on the crockpot, so the dinner you were expecting is still raw, and you end up serving cereal for dinner.

I say all of that to say this—the level of perfection we expect from ourselves sometimes, only belongs to Christ. And though as women, as humans, we will always fall short, God will cover any of our lack with His grace. Paul affirmed this in 2 Corinthians 12:9, "My grace is sufficient for you, for my power is made perfect in weakness." If God's power is on full display and brought to completion *in our weaknesses,* then why in the world are we trying so hard to do it all on our own? That Scripture should be our mic drop moment when we read it, sis. It tells us all we need to know. We weren't meant to bear the image of perfection; we were created to bear the image of Christ.

You see, friend, I had spent so much time planning out the perfect outfits for the perfect family picture. The coordinating colors, the matchy bows, suspenders, and stockings. I lost myself in Pinterest boards. And in all the planning for the perfect picture, I'd lost sight of the bigger picture. I lost sight of what really mattered that morning. The fact that I had arrived at church with my five healthy babies. The family that I had prayed so hard for over the years was finally a reality. My husband and I had battled infertility and had been through IVF countless times to finally have the family we had always dreamed of. I was *living out* answered prayers.

As I began to look at those sweet chubby cheeks and that grin the size of Texas, all that disappointment over the missing Easter outfit began to fade. It was soon replaced with my laughter. Laughter is the best medicine for the soul. It was a reminder for me to let go of any idea of perfection that I had in mind. The perfect outfit. The perfect picture. None of that really mattered. What truly mattered was right in front of me.

Jesus simply doesn't care about all the fluff. He doesn't care if we come to Him in our fancy outfits or in our tattered, dirty dinosaur pajamas. He just wants us to show up. He already knows our hearts. He knows us better than we know ourselves. Every joy, every source of pain, every worry, every fear, every last insecurity. Our dreams and our hearts' greatest desires. He knows each and every one.

Here's another thing about God, He is never surprised when things don't go our way, but He is always there to redirect us to the bigger picture. That Easter morning, His sweet reminder to me was that the bigger picture had nothing to do with the picture I had planned. It looked more like surrender. Gratefulness. Embracing the chaos that went along with my big, beautiful family. It looked like leaning more into Jesus.

May we never forget to see the bigger picture. *God never asked us to be flawless. He asks us to be faithful.* You see, flawless can't handle pressure. Being flawless is all about image, but one mistake can shatter an image. Being faithful is all about obedience. Being faithful looks like resetting the tone of the day with prayer and inviting God into our messes. Faithful beats flawless every single day. Especially on Easter Sunday when you show up with your child in dirty pajamas.

I know that this specific story is very insignificant and lighthearted compared to other disappointments we may face in life. Sometimes it's the things that leave a bigger scar and mark on our lives:

- The friendship you had to mourn because that person hurt you and betrayed you deeply.
- Chronic pain from an illness that leaves you feeling drained and defeated.
- The weight of financial debt that you don't see a way out of, and it robs you of enjoying your everyday life.

- Watching someone you love battle addiction and no matter how hard you're fighting for them, you end up disappointed.
- The one pink line when you are desperately praying each month to see two of them. Infertility has an excruciating way of leaving disappointment as an imprint on your heart and mind.

We have all battled our own disappointments.

Here is what I've learned about disappointment. It is never wanted, but in the same way, it's never wasted. None of us add "disappointment" to our prayer list. It's not something we wish or pray for. But in the moments we find ourselves in the midst of it, God will absolutely bring purpose from it.

God just wants us to come to Him as we are. Not perfect. Not polished or put together. Just come to Him—dirty dinosaur pajamas and all. Dump out the worries that are weighing you down and give it to Jesus. He'll give you peace in return, and I'll take peace over perfection any day.

Purpose doesn't require polish,

IT REQUIRES PRESENCE.

Identity Crisis

An alternative title for this chapter is, "The Time I Colored My Hair Blue."

I had just turned thirty-one during Covid lockdowns. I was in a season of exclusive breastfeeding, and and life was feeling a little heavier than normal. This was before we began our homeschool journey, and we were adapting to virtual school at home. Zoom meetings in my chaotic household were enough ammunition alone for a *full nervous breakdown*. Normalcy had hopped on a midnight train to another universe, with no return in sight. Looking back, dyeing my hair blue was definitely my version of a 2007 Britney meltdown.

But before we go any further, I want you to know something. I am not making light of all of the terrible aftermath and effects that came from Covid. To be transparent, Covid changed everything. It was heavy, it was beyond stressful, and life-altering. I most certainly do not take that lightly. Oftentimes, life is heavy enough in itself. Being able to look back on hard times with a little humor helps us to breathe again (figuratively and literally) and also reflect on the silver linings that came from the other side of the mask.

The silver linings that specific year came wrapped in masks, cancelled plans, Zoom calls, hand sanitizer, and toilet paper panic buys. It was a time that forced us to slow down and be at home. All of our plans came to a halt, and we were forced to spend time with our family within the walls of our homes.

My family took walks together again, a habit we'd long forgotten about. We brought back the lost art of a family dinner as we gathered around the table together. Our kids even got bored for the first time in a long time. All our seemingly important plans were cancelled. But we also had to tread in the waters of the unknown.

Yes, we also had to deal with masks and endless fearmongering. Though it was a quiet time, the diverse opinions echoed so loudly it would give anyone a headache. There were so many voices, so many opinions. We had to make impossible decisions about vaccines that impacted our lives, jobs, and health. I think most of us learned during that time that you cannot fully trust in any political party or any government. Instead, you have to do your own research and trust in the only Being that is 100% trustworthy in questionable times—Jesus.

Essentially, much of our everyday lives in 2020 were turned completely upside down. Covid most certainly made people completely re-evaluate every aspect of their lives. Many people even had some sort of identity crisis during Covid. *Close your eyes for just a minute and envision your sister over here with the blue hair.*

It was my birthday. Not the exciting/depressing milestone—the one that came after the infamous thirtieth birthday. I was feeling a little depressed and in search of some sort of excitement in my life. I'd also been cooped up in our house for days and was slightly losing my mind. It wasn't just Covid that created an open door for an identity crisis. My youngest baby Tillie had hit a growth spurt and was nursing every hour. My older kids' appetites increased from boredom, and I was so tired of trying to figure out what to fix for every meal. And my marriage was on the rocks.

So often, we place our identity in things that were never meant to hold our identity. Our jobs, our husbands, our kids. I know I did, especially in this challenging season of life. Maybe it was something else that made you lose your spark:

- Postpartum depression
- Loss of a job
- Divorce
- Infertility
- Betrayal
- Motherhood
- Co-dependency
- Unrealistic expectations

We so often look to our external circumstances to fix this deep need we have for identity. *If I'm the perfect mom, then I won't feel so miserable. If I can just get my dream job, then I'll feel worthy. If I dye my hair blue, I'll like what I see in the mirror.* These self-deceptions often leave us worn out and hungry for more. Deception has haunted women since the beginning of, well, womanhood, and the only way to fight against them is to place your identity in the only Being that can meet your need to be seen, known, and loved fully just as you are.

The Attack on Women Since the Beginning

There is a spiritual attack on the identity of women. Me, you, your sister, your mom, your grandmother. All of us women. But this attack isn't anything new. It seems as if Satan has been in the most aggressive game of attacking women relentlessly since the beginning of time—throwing fiery darts of lies and deception all throughout our lives. To unpack all of this, I think we need to grasp the significance of a woman. Let's go back to the very first one: Eve.

The very existence of women alone makes hell nervous. Since the beginning of time, there has been an attack on the *woman* and the *womb*. As I was in prayer about this very topic recently, God nudged me to go back and study in Genesis. I realized that there are only a few verses between the creation of Eve and the fall. Satan wasted no time trying to dismantle what God had intricately and intentionally created.

In Genesis 2:22-23 it says, "Then the Lord God made a woman from the rib he had taken out of the man, and he brought her to the man. The man said, 'This is now bone of my bones and flesh of my flesh; she shall be called "woman" for she was taken out of man.'"

There are only two verses between creation of woman and Satan's scheme to attack.

Two verses out of 31,102 that a New International Version Bible contains. Genesis 3:1 says, "Now the serpent was more crafty than any of the wild animals the Lord God has made. He said to the woman, "Did God *really* say, 'You must not eat from any tree in the garden'?" So why did the creation of a woman make Satan waste no time pouncing?

Interestingly enough, the name Eve means "life." Eve was the mother of all the living. You see, friend, sometimes we may view this story as Eve being an afterthought. But that's simply not true. She was part of the plan the entire time. We all came about from the life and creation of Eve. Even Jesus. Eve's son, Seth, became an ancestor of our Messiah. It was through a womb that Jesus, our Savior, was born.

All throughout Scripture, time after time, God chose women to do such significant things for the kingdom and for mankind.

- Mary, chosen to be the mother of Jesus
- Esther, chosen to be a queen who saved her people
- Mary Magdalene, chosen to follow Jesus and finance His ministry on earth

I am fully convinced that few things bring the enemy more joy and satisfaction than when he distracts God's daughters from walking in their God-given identity. Because it is then that he has a foothold, a method of delaying us from walking in purpose. The enemy hates what he fears, and he most definitely fears what God uses to bring forth redemption and carry life. He also knows that as soon as we become mothers (physically and/or spiritually), that we become an even bigger threat.

You see, sister, that apple didn't satisfy. It may have looked delicious, beautiful, and shiny. It may have seemed enticing, yet it carried consequences that Eve could not grasp. In this same way, Satan still dresses distractions in appealing ways. He wraps them up in pretty paper with a big, shiny bow, all while keeping the destruction tucked underneath, hidden from your sight. Not everything that's pretty and shiny is sacred. Satan sends us on endless chases that just leave us panting for water and completely out of breath.

We chase after things that will never fulfill us:

- Busy Schedules
- The Perfect Career
- Perfection
- Endless Productivity
- Comparison
- The Perfect Home

He makes all of these things look good, like shiny things that we are naturally drawn to. He makes them look a lot like "success" or "happiness." When we spend our years chasing after all of these things, we just end up exhausted, worn thin, broke, and left with a void that none of those things will ever fill. Once Satan sends us on a wild goose chase after all of these things, he has us right where he wants us.

Distractions > Deception > Delay

The enemy is the father of lies. In Genesis 3, he deceives Eve by responding to her refusal of the fruit by saying, *"Did God really say . . .?"* Don't we still see him using these very same schemes in today's generation?

- Are you really enough?
- Why is she so successful and you aren't?
- Are you really supposed to fight for your marriage?
- Does God really hear all your prayers?

Here's the thing I want you to know, sweet friend, distraction often-times begins with deception. And those very deceptions can lead to destruction and delay. You see, when sin entered the game, it didn't cancel God's plan. He still had the victory, but it sure did cause a lot of heartache in between.

Eve fell into the tricks and schemes of the enemy and ate the apple. Not because Eve was weak, but because she was human. The apple looked shiny and beautiful, and she chose to ignore God's clear commands. This very act led to the fall of creation and sin. When I think of this story in the Bible, it's like watching a movie unfold. Knowing what's coming makes me want to shout in slow motion, "Noooo, donnnnn't eatttt ittttt." Especially after it brought the curse of painful menstrual cycles and childbirth. After experiencing the excruciating pain of childbirth from my six babies, I really wish she'd left it alone. *For real, Eve? Girl, that about took me out, literally.* They say you forget the pain, but I've found that to be a lie!

Though it would have been lovely to live in a world without maxi pads and with pain-free childbirth, I can't help but have compassion for Eve. Because I myself have fallen for the enemy's tactics too many times to count. His sneaky whispers and lies may be quiet, but they've echoed through the chambers of our hearts as women, more often than we'd like to admit.

They sound a lot like:

"You are too broken to ever be fixed."

"God isn't going to come through for you."

"You need more to be satisfied."

Even though I know that I am covered in the blood of Jesus and have all power and authority over every lie, every scheme, and every tactic,

I'm still human and struggle at times. I was raised up knowing the truth and believing the truth. But those truths are harder at times to grasp once you get older. Especially when the waves of life leave you constantly treading to keep your head above water.

Sister, I have been there. I've been in those waters of survival and self-doubt. So many of us have. You aren't alone, even in seasons where you're tired and the water is cold and so dark that you can barely see in front of you. As I'm writing this, tears have fallen as I've pictured so many women in dark waters. I've imagined a similar scene from the *Titanic*. When the ship is sinking and the water is freezing and so many are giving up because they don't see any way out.

There are so many moments that we find ourselves gasping for air beneath the waves of fear, worry, anxiety, self-doubt. This is my hope and prayer: for you to know that when you find your head barely above the water and exhausted from the treading, there is a life preserver. There is a hand reaching out towards you to pull you out of those waters. I can't stand to see someone suffering, and so many women do it silently. I've imagined myself throwing you a buoy, a life preserver, to help pull you out. But Jesus—He is the life preserver. When you reach towards Him in those moments when you're drowning, His grace will keep you afloat.

You see, friend, *hope is not found in how hard you swim. It's found in who you choose to reach for in those moments.*

Clinging to lies that Satan whispers, won't save you. Labels like "not enough", "too much", "forgotten," will only pull you further under. When we choose to cling to Jesus, He replaces every lie and every false identity with His truth:

You are redeemed.

You are loved.

You are chosen.

Comparison and Contentment

John 10:10 says, "The thief comes only to steal and kill and destroy; I have come that they may have life and life abundantly." Satan has mastered the very things he knows best:

Lies.

Deception.

Robbing us of joy.

I don't know about you, but when I look in the mirror, it's as if I am wearing special tunnel vision goggles. The kind that illuminates my insecurities. It's as if every flaw on my body is supernaturally highlighted in my brain. I see the wrinkles, the cellulite, the stretch marks. I see age spots on my chest and a little extra skin under my arms. Can you relate?

Growing up, it used to be magazines that we would pass in the grocery store that we compared ourselves to. But now, those comparisons are always at our fingertips. As soon as we open our social media feed, images to compare ourselves to are literally everywhere.

Throughout our days, Satan whispers lies that cause us to doubt our own self-worth.

"You will never be good enough,"
"Everyone is gossiping about you."
"Look at her, she has her life so much more together than you ever will."
"If you don't look like her, live like her, parent like her, organize like her, then you're a failure."

We have all fallen victim to the lies that the enemy whispers. That we are small and insignificant. *That someone else's highlight reel is real life.* We often forget that the serpent needs to go back where he belongs. Under our feet. Crushed. Defeated. He has no place in our thoughts, minds, or hearts. The Bible legit tells us to take *every* thought captive for a reason.

Hear me out—this is *not* a chapter about bashing any of the women we may compare ourselves to. This isn't about jealousy; it's about human nature. The women on social media are not the enemy. In fact, I can bet that most of them are just doing their best too.

And can I tell you a secret?

They may just be comparing themselves to you too.

They have their own insecurities too.

Maybe comparison happens at the gym with the girl working out next to you. She looks strong and steady. She also looks like she came out of a fitness magazine and she most certainly hasn't had sweets in ten years. Instead of keeping your eyes on the elliptical, or letting her inspire you, you secretly want to force feed her a chocolate donut.

Perhaps it's the social butterfly of your small town. She constantly seems to be having fun. Out on the town at fun dinners and social events, while you're at home washing dishes, while wearing your husband's oversized T-shirt.

Or maybe it's the influencer on your social media feed. The one with thousands of followers. Her photos are bright and perfect, and she seems to be too. Her home is immaculate and clean and her walls are white. Meanwhile, you have crayon marks and scribbles on yours and your paint hasn't been updated in ten years. Or you may even have a few holes in the drywall because your children love to wrestle—acting out their own WWE fights in every room of your house. Ok, I'll admit it, that last one was all me and my house.

So what do we do when we find ourselves stuck in a cycle of comparison? We shift our focus. None of those women are the problem. The problem is that we turn all of that comparison into a mental competition we create all on our own. And we view ourselves as behind in a race we were never even meant to be in. The only competition I want to be in is with myself last week. And not in a toxic, negative way. But in a way that pushes me to work towards my goals and makes me reflect back on how far I've come. Instead of feeling somehow threatened or inadequate by someone else's successes, workout routine, or organization skills, we should celebrate their wins too. There will always be comparisons in life, no matter what they may be. But we have to fix our eyes on who is above us, not who is beside us. Our performance does not affect our purpose.

Here's something I am learning: comparison cannot thrive in a content heart. Contentment is a choice and it's something we have to choose every single day. Something I've learned in my thirties is that paid off looks so much better to me than brand new. Just recently my husband mentioned browsing for a new vehicle soon. I instantly objected. I've come to love my large twelve-passenger van, even if it embarrasses my daughter when I pick her up from practice. Even if it's missing some hubcaps and has several dents in the bumper, or the fact that sometimes my sun visor dangles from the ceiling if I take a sharp turn. I may have had it for seven years, but it's paid for. It gets us where we're going, and there is most definitely plenty of room.

The thing is, with any material thing, the new wears off.

The fresh highlights grow out.

The new outfit is great until you get a coffee stain on it.

The new phone is only the newest model for a few months until a newer, better one comes out on the market.

We have to stop chasing the carrot on a stick that just leaves us feeling frustrated and unsatisfied. If we hinge our happiness on temporal things like achievements, titles, social status, appearance, or applause, we will only be left feeling empty and exhausted.

It's like eating endless amounts of junk food when we are hungry. When what we really need is a meal instead. It will just leave us feeling bloated and blah because we need substance.

I've learned to choose to be content with the season and circumstances I'm in, in every season because God's in it with me. This is easier to do when we choose to see how blessed we truly are. Cultivating gratitude goes a long way.

Take a minute and reflect on your life. Are you currently living in answered prayers?

There is a sign that hangs in my living room that says, "I still remember the days I prayed for what I have now." It's so true and so convicting at times. We don't have time for comparison when we are busy focusing on the amazing blessings right in front of us.

My sink may be full of dishes, but my kids' bellies are full.

The laundry may be piling up, but that means that my kids have plenty of clothes.

My home may be full of noise, but it's even more full of love.

Gratitude doesn't mean pretending it's easy; it means refusing to view my many blessings as burdens in any way.

Take Every Thought Captive

When we feel our eyes start to drift, we must remember to hold tight to something that the Bible very clearly advises in Philippians 4:8, "*Finally, brothers and sisters, whatever is true, whatever is noble, whatever is right, whatever is pure, whatever is lovely, whatever is admirable—if anything is excellent or praiseworthy—think about such things.*"

A couple of years ago, my friend was struggling badly with her mental health. She had been battling depression and anxiety, and her marriage was on the rocks. Life wasn't quite going as she had planned for herself or her family. At that time, she and I were in similar seasons with our rollercoasters of emotions, and we had become each other's confidantes and prayer warriors. We would, and we still do, send texts on days that are seemingly extra hard or when we find ourselves in a funk. A lot of times, I may not have wisdom to offer, but I have an ear to listen. And I would often respond with, "I totally understand how you are feeling, I've been there." We all need that kind of friend in life.

One particular morning was especially hard for her that year and she sent a text pleading for prayer to get through the morning. As I was praying for her, the Holy Spirit prompted me to message and tell her about a practical step to take. And I feel like I need to share the same message with you today:

> *"I'm gonna tell you something that may seem silly, but it does help me. Claim biblical truths and affirmations out loud:*
> *I am the head and not the tail.*
> *I am above and not beneath.*
> *Greater is He that is in me than he who is in the world.*
> *I rebuke and I silence any lies from the enemy to try and derail me from God's purpose.*
> *The devil is a liar, and no weapon formed against me will prosper.*
> *My future years will be greater than my former years.*
> *I plead the blood of Jesus over my family, my marriage, my children, and my mind."*

I want you to speak these aloud too. Boldly declare all of these truths and apply them to your own life. Write them on your mirror. Do what my friend did—print them out and hang them as reminders all around your home. The only way to crush the lie is to crush the serpent's head, the father of all lies. When the enemy tempts you to compare yourself to another woman, beat yourself up, or dwell on what you don't have, show him everything you do have. And what you have is better. Peace. Contentment. Joy. Gratitude. Grace.

Placing Identity in God's Love for You

Jesus is the most perfect example of pure, unconditional love. No strings attached. The thing is that we don't have to live *for* God's love. Not for His approval, His acceptance, or His admiration. We can live our lives in a position *from* all of those things.

There is a Greek word that was often used in ancient times on receipts to indicate that a debt had been "fully paid." In a judicial context for courts, it was also used to indicate that a sentence was "fully served." The price that Jesus paid wasn't cheap; it was paid in full by His precious, innocent blood. When Jesus spoke His last words when He was crucified on the cross for us, He said "Tetelestai." *It is finished.* No more need to work for or earn God's grace, no more barriers to His presence; in that moment, humanity once again had direct access to God—like Adam and Eve did in the Garden of Eden. All was made right.

As a mother, I know, without any hesitation that my children could never, ever do anything in their power to make me stop loving them. In the same way, Romans 8:38-39 instructs us of this, "For I am convinced that neither death, nor life, neither angels, nor demons, neither the present nor the future, nor any powers, neither height nor depth, nor anything else in all creation, will be able to separate us from the love of God that is in Christ Jesus our Lord." If I, Andi, *in all of my flaws and imperfections*, know without a doubt that this is the truth, then why would we ever question the fact that this does not apply to me as well? I have no doubt that our heavenly Father looks at us in the same loving ways that we look at our daughters and sons.

We may see tired eyes, yesterday's makeup, stretch marks, and stretched thin places. We may see the list of things we haven't yet completed, the laundry piles that seem to keep growing and unwashed dishes. Lots of dishes. We place focus on our every flaw and shortcoming; God sees us in a radically different perspective. You're not just a mom to Him. You aren't just a wife. You are His daughter first.

He sees you exactly as you are, and He looks at you through eyes of compassion and grace.

He sees a faithful servant.

He sees beauty in your brokenness.

I know it breaks His heart to see us tear ourselves apart, like we do far too often. I know this because He spoke to my heart about this a few months ago while preparing for a message at a women's conference.

I had known about this specific conference for months and I had been praying and prepping my message. The week before the conference,

I felt like I was hitting a wall. I prayed and cried out to God and the only response I got in return was silence. We all go through these seasons, and I'm not a stranger to those feelings. I am strong in my faith, and I know that feelings aren't fact. However, my flesh wanted to scream and cry and throw a tantrum on the floor. I'm not proud to admit that I may or may not have done a couple of those things. But I kept pressing and I kept praying and finally by Wednesday of that week, I had my answer. The Lord broke the silence in the kindest and gentlest way. It reminded me of the times as parents, when we wait on our kids to stop whining and throwing a fit before we speak. We've all been there. It's in those moments when we know that they won't comprehend what we are explaining until they calm themselves down and listen. So I did. He said, "You need to renounce any lies that *you* have come into agreement with from the enemy about your own worth."

Ironically, I was speaking on self-worth and identity, yet I was still struggling with both of those things. I was guilty of allowing the enemy to slap me around with little whispers that sounded like this:

"You will never be enough."
"You are too messy to minister to anyone."
"You will never be healed."
"Are you sure God called you to this?"

The enemy was working hard to distract me and make me question my identity and worth, and in doing so, make me question God and His Word. This is his first step to delaying us from walking out into our purpose. The best way to fight off the lies is to remember that God is with you all the time and He wants to fight every identity crisis with you.

Getting that blue out of my hair was kind of a nightmare; ask the sweet hairstylist that spent hours stripping it. How often do we find ourselves in a mess that is completely, 100% by our own doing, just like Eve; and it takes a long time to get rid of the mess we made. For months, I still found traces of blue. Even on my pillowcase.

But lean into this, sister—anytime that we build our identity on our circumstances, it will always come crumbling down. Always. But when our identity is rooted in Christ, it is steady. Not easily shaken and it most certainly *cannot* be shifted. You see, even when my hair was blue (praise God it was short-lived), it may have changed my appearance, but it never once changed who I was. I was still a daughter of God. I still had purpose even though I had a hard time finding exactly what that was. I was still His daughter, and I was still chosen and loved—blue hair and all.

My purpose isn't hiding on the other side of perfection. IT'S RIGHT THERE, WOVEN INTO THE ORDINARY, waiting for me to embrace it instead of apologizing for it."

Walking in Your Purpose

own a laminator. Nothing fancy. No bells and whistles, but it does the job. When I use it, I feel as though I have my life together in some strange sense. Even though my entire house may be in shambles, if I laminate a piece of artwork or a Christmas craft for a family member, all feels right in my world. I admitted this false feeling to my teenage daughter and laughter erupted out of her like lava out of a volcano. Because she knows the truth: I most definitely do not have my life together.

I've always heard people reference Type A people. I don't know much about what makes each personality trait be uniquely wired this way, but I do know this much: I'm wired differently. God must have run out of type A wires when He knit me in my momma's womb. I like to call myself a type Z. The opposite of whatever a type A is. I wish my brain was wired that way, but it simply is not. Surprisingly enough, my middle daughter, Cozi, is very detail-oriented, organized, and helps her momma find her keys daily. For years, and even now at times, I struggle with being a type Z. Especially when it comes to juggling schedules for the eight of us in the house. ADHD does not help matters either.

My children are very active members of 4-H. They are creative and amazing public speakers. They always do very well with competition in surrounding counties and have even won state competitions. And that is all *in spite* of their unorganized mother.

Last year while at a regional competition I walked into the room full of highly prepared mothers and felt like I was in one of those dreams where you have to give a speech to the school naked. You know those? No? Ok, well never mind. Didn't mean to make it weird. But if you do know those kinds of dreams of sheer panic and anxiety, that's exactly how I felt. Unprepared. Insecurity seeped into every part of me. Like it came from a leaky water hose that couldn't be fixed. No matter how much duct tape suffocated the leak, it spewed out anyways.

As I scanned the room, I clutched the side of my trusty 4-H bag tightly. The bag, just like the laminator, gave me some odd, false sense of "having it together." Even if it was the smallest bit. My sweet, supportive sister-in-law smirked as I admitted this confession to her.

As I gripped tightly to my bag, a crunch from the inside broke the silence of the room. I peered into the bag hoping the culprit was some sort of tool that would help me prepare my children a little bit more or perhaps a sign I could hold up that said, "I know I'm a mess, but my children belong in this room," but all that I found was a few extra random notecards and a small bag of *now crushed* Doritos. I had remembered to grab a snack on the way out the door when I heard my growing man child mention that he was hungry (even though he'd already eaten). But those crushed Doritos weren't going to help me feel any bit secure at that moment. Perhaps I would have felt better if I darted to the bathroom and scarfed them down myself.

Even though I had spent weeks helping my babies practice and get ready, I am just not the one that comes in with the labeled totes, and I'm most definitely not the one to arrive thirty minutes early for any occasion. I felt very insignificant and began to scan the room and subconsciously began to compare myself to all the other moms. And to be clear, there was nothing wrong with the organized moms. If anything, I admire them. But all I could see in that quiet and crowded classroom was everything that I was not.

Neat.

Professional.

Organized.

My daughter had been practicing for days on her charcuterie board for her food demonstration, and I was her right-hand gal. There for support and anything she needed. I helped chop and wash veggies and reminded her when she needed to make more eye contact. And in case you were wondering, *I did* laminate her recipes she'd printed for the judges, so that they wouldn't get wrinkled. Wrinkled like my outfit I threw on as I rushed out the door, carrying posters bigger than me.

That night was a frazzled mess for me. But a beautiful one. My daughter and son both won that night, in spite of their unorganized momma. In the midst of the rush and the chaos, I let comparison steal my joy. I didn't reflect on the countless nights that I had stayed up timing their speeches the weeks prior. I seemed to forget all of the dishes I had washed each night from practicing their recipes. And what about the handwritten notes that I had spent so much time on to help them each remember their speeches. It slipped my mind the blazers I had pressed so that they would be neatly dressed for their contests.

(Ok. Wait. Hold up before we move on. I'm not a fraud so I have to clarify this before I move on. I don't press anything unless it is with my flat iron. Yes, I am being serious. I accidentally (or purposefully) threw away my iron years ago. Please don't tell my great-aunt who purchased it for us as a wedding gift.)

You see, my purpose isn't to be the most organized person in the world. I would fail at that every single day, multiple times. My purpose is found in mothering my six beautiful children and supporting them as they grow. If I put my focus on someone else's skill set or if I take on someone else's purpose as my own, then I will fall short and lose sight of the identity and purpose God has called me to.

I don't need to master color-coded calendars or wake up before dawn to prove my worth. I don't need a perfectly curated life to be living on purpose. The calling God placed on my life fits the chaos I'm already standing in—it meets me in carpool lines, in unfinished laundry, in the holy work of showing up again and again when I'm tired. Purpose doesn't require polish; it requires presence.

And when I remember that—when I release the pressure to become someone I was never meant to be—I can breathe again. I can stop measuring myself against standards God never set and start trusting that He knew exactly what He was doing when He gave *this* life to *me*. My purpose isn't hiding on the other side of perfection. It's right here, woven into the ordinary, waiting for me to embrace it instead of apologize for it.

Purpose in the Mundane

I know, from deep within my bones, that motherhood is the greatest ministry that I will ever do. God has given me so many opportunities to do ministry on platforms, podcasts, and stages, and even through this book. And I'm so incredibly grateful, because He knows that I have a fire that burns for ministry and sharing the love of Jesus in every capacity possible.

So I am so incredibly grateful for every door God opens for me to do just that. But before any of that, my number one ministry He's given me is within the walls of my home. It is the *highest* and *holiest* of callings.

It's in the mundane tasks like wiping tears and wiping counters. It's in packing lunches and tending to boo-boos. It's in the grocery trips and the endless meals you cook for your family. It's in the middle of the night prayers that no one hears but you and God.

This is the kingdom work that gets no applause.

But even in the mundane, this work is holy. *Because, ultimately, the mundane is the heart of motherhood.* Sometimes we forget that. We find ourselves getting discouraged in our everyday motherhood tasks. We convince ourselves that it matters less. The enemy tries to sneak in so he can whisper lies to convince you that the middle and the mundane don't matter.

Have you ever wondered why Satan attacks mothers in these kinds of seasons?

He will try to steal your joy through depression, anxiety, or distractions. He will pull out every tactic to make you feel isolated and lonely. He will try to pull wool over your eyes so that it's hard to see the blessings right in front of you.

It's because Satan knows. He knows what we forget sometimes when we are overwhelmed and exhausted. He knows that motherhood is our number one mission field. He knows that is our most important ministry. And that alone makes him shake in his boots. The ministry of a Christian mother makes hell nervous. So he wants you to feel unimportant and unseen.

It makes me think of Hagar in the Bible. Hagar was a foreign slave who ultimately felt invisible and worthless. She was forced by Sarah, her master, to have a child with Abraham due to Sarah's infertility. When Hagar obeyed and got pregnant, she then faced severe mistreatment due to Sarah's jealousy. Sarah made Hagar's life so difficult that she ran away into the desert. She was running with an unknown future and destination. She felt tapped out. Done. At the end of her rope. She had a pivotal moment in the desert when she encountered an angel that God had sent her to offer her a solution. It gave her peace and reassurance that God would bless her and provide for her and her son.

Genesis 16:13 says, "She gave this name to the Lord who spoke to her: "You are the God who sees me," for she said, "I have now seen the one who sees me." She gave God the name El Roi, which means the God who sees me. You see, Hagar was a slave, a surrogate, a concubine, a runaway. But yet, God knew her. God heard her. God *saw* her.

And the same God that saw Hagar sees you too.

Hidden doesn't mean insignificant.

Maybe you've been there too, momma.

Wandering in a wilderness of your own, feeling hopeless and lonely.

But God finds you and He meets you right there.

Because He is the God who sees.

The work of motherhood may look mundane to the world, but it is significant to God.

Because He is the God who sees. He sees all that you do for your family. All the sacrifices. All the little things that culture tries to tell you won't measure up to much. Heaven applauds each of them more so than the tasks of a CEO at a multi-million-dollar company. Because you're shepherding hearts and souls, momma. And you're doing it so well.

And here's the thing about parenting: it's a process. But one that holds so much purpose. And in a world full of shortcuts, there is no shortcut or hack when it comes to being a mother and raising a family. There isn't a code you can crack for shaping a human heart that God has entrusted you with. There's just faithfulness over and over again. And grace, lots of grace.

Abiding in the Giver of Our Purpose

Raising kids requires us to stay connected to God. My kids don't just need my best efforts. Because anything I do on my own strength gets me nowhere. Motherhood doesn't just require effort; it requires abiding.

John 15:5 says, "I am the vine and you are the branches. Whoever abides in me and I in him, will bear much fruit; apart from me you can do nothing" (ESV). You see, we cannot pour out what we aren't receiving. If I try to bear my own fruits, they'll be all moldy, rotten, and bitter. Yuck. They'll manifest as anger, bitterness, impatience. All of these rotten fruits stem from trying to do it all on our own human strength while fueled by too much caffeine, stress, and exhaustion.

But if I abide in Christ and stay connected to the vine, I will bear the Fruit of the Spirit. Joy. Patience. Goodness. Gentleness. Self-control. This may not happen overnight but when we spend time with God through prayer and through reading His Word, His character begins to rub off on us.

When writing this section, I was reminded of a social media post I made last year. It said, "How does one bear the fruits of the spirit while parenting teenagers?" This post seemed to be both relatable and laughable to other mommas like me who were in a similar season. I still struggle today, but on those days that are extra hard, I ask myself if I have been abiding? Or if I have been trying to parent my own way on my own strength?

In the warmer months, I start my day before my kids get up with a prayer walk. It is intentional time with God to pray about everything before my day begins. I cannot tell you just how much that small habit changed my life for the better. Sometimes in the winter I might be a little extra snappy, since those walks don't happen much in that season, so I have to be more intentional then. Something else I love to do is prayer journals. Write down Scriptures to declare over my family. I have journals from years ago that I have went back to and checked off answered prayers that I'm currently living out.

And I wanna pause for a minute and speak to the momma that is tired. You may be at a point in this chapter where you're rolling your eyes a little bit at the idea of journaling or worse, getting up early to go walk. I get it, sister. I really do. I've been there and I understand your hesitation and your exhaustion. But I do want to emphasize that I didn't mention running one time, and you will never ever see me running unless something is chasing me. I hate to run. Just a slow, self-paced walk. A walk with intentional prayer time. Even if it's out in the yard or your driveway. It doesn't have to be anything crazy. But try it for a week and let me know how you feel.

Something else that helps me to abide is inviting my babies into everyday rhythms. Pray together. Listen to worship music together. Read and recite Scriptures together. Teach them Psalms 23 and then go celebrate with blizzards from Dairy Queen. Little things like that stick with them for life. And they can tuck away those Scriptures on their hearts and save them for hard times down the road when they will need them the most.

Being intentional and authentic in motherhood *is everything.*

I never want my motherhood to be based on performance, mine or my kids'.

We all have moments where we are so incredibly proud and others where we feel like a complete failure. There are days that are just plain hard. Days when we can't seem to get anything right.

Instead, of measuring my motherhood against an unattainable standard, I want it based on authenticity. My goal and prayer daily is to be the kind of mom that abides more than I perform or try to do it on my own, without full reliance on Christ. Authenticity means being completely transparent along the way. It means apologizing in the moments that I get it wrong. But it also means pointing them back to God in real time. Every moment, every day. The good, the bad, and the messy (which is pretty much every day at my house). We aren't robots, we all are just doing the best we can. God gives us new chances and new mercies each morning.

We have to remind ourselves that we are a branch but not the vine. Our babies don't need perfect mommas; they just need connected moms who know where their strength comes from.

Your Words Shape Your Purpose

Growing up, my nana always warned "if you speak it, it will come to you."

It is true that the power of life and death is in the tongue.

I have a podcast that I pray over before I release each episode. It's full of encouragement for other moms like me. The words are dripping with grace, but I often leave none for myself. Isn't that what we do sometimes? We hold conversations and space and love for other people in our lives but we put our own self-doubts to the side. We build up others but tear ourselves down. We speak affirmations but find ourselves believing that those same truths don't apply to us. We have to break this toxic cycle. Maybe we didn't choose to feel this way but we do get to choose how to deal with those feelings. Have you ever heard the saying about parenting, "Do as I say, not as I do?" Well, that's malarky. Malarky . . . did I just say that word? I'll go ahead and see myself out (my teenagers would definitely say I am a "boomer" for using that word.)

The point is, lectures don't stick. And sister, while raising teenagers, I have wasted a lot of my breath doing *just that*. Lecturing. Trying to get my point across. Tirelessly explaining. Over and over again. And yet, so often, my words seemed to be wasted breath. Yes, words matter, but they also need to be *lived out*. It's not about saying the right words; it's about demonstrating truth and virtue in our everyday lives. Living it out. You see, our kids see us. They see our trials and our triumphs. They also see how we apply our own words to our own lives. And if we don't live it out, how can we expect them to do the same?

Only You Can Walk Out Your Purpose

I wish I could invite you into my messy house; I would push the laundry basket to the side and offer you a cup of coffee. I would love to sit face to face with you and tell you this: I know it isn't easy. But we owe it to ourselves to stop the cycle of self-destruction from the way that we view ourselves. Ahemmm, as I clear my throat here in this moment, I am talking to myself too. Yet again.

Momma, you are worthy.

Because you are His too.

And he created you for such a time as this.

Ephesians 2:10 tells us, "We are God's masterpiece. He has created us anew in Christ Jesus, so we can do the good things he planned for us long ago" (NLT). Yes, you are God's masterpiece. It may sound cheesy or cliché, and you may, at times, struggle to believe it. But it is the absolute truth. I feel like I'm the kind of masterpiece that has been super glued over and over and I may even have some brightly colored, wrinkled-up duct tape holding me together. But I can hold on to the truth in Psalms 139 that says,

"For you created my inmost being; you knit me together in my mother's womb. I praise you because I am fearfully and wonderfully made; your works are wonderful, I know that full well." He knows every single hair, every wrinkle, every scar. Every freckle and each stretch mark.

I'm reminded of Psalm 139 when I look at my own beautiful daughters. I want so badly for them to believe all of the things that God says they are.

Beautiful.

Chosen.

Perfectly Loved.

My oldest daughter struggles with this at times. No matter how many reminders she gets, it's still a truth she struggles with. My own mother would tell you the same thing about me. Even as an adult, my mom keeps me in check when I seem to forget to apply these truths to my own life. How can we teach our daughters to love themselves, when we find that nearly impossible to do ourselves?

I'm also reminded that I am God's daughter. Me. The thirty-six-year-old momma of six.

I'm not just a short-order cook, a chauffeur, a maid (not a very good one at that). Not only am I a chaos coordinator, I'm not only a homeschool teacher or a wrestling referee to my wild boys. I'm not *just* a wife to my husband. Our motherhood is not defined by our tasks. It isn't defined by all the things we don't get done for the day. It's defined in our identity as God's children.

Ralph Waldo Emerson has a quote that says, "To be yourself in a world that is constantly trying to make you something else is the greatest accomplishment." God created you as His masterpiece and He has a plan for your life. So now is the time that you have to choose to speak more kindly to yourself. Day in and day out. The easy days and definitely on the really tough ones. It starts with us. We cannot expect our daughters to have a healthy self-image if we keep hopping on the rusty bicycle of broken down worth and shattered self-esteem. We know that that particular bike breaks down easily and leaves us scraped up on the ground.

Something that I'm learning is that contentment, specifically when it comes to body image, has nothing to do with a number on a scale but it lies within our hearts. Recently, I started doing something called intermittent fasting. I was doing it more for health benefits, to reduce inflammation and pain. My mother battles multiple health issues and she has passed a couple of those down to me. With that, I also started daily exercise. I did feel so much better, both physically and emotionally. The number on the scale also began to drop. And hey, it's swimsuit season, so I wasn't mad about it! However, I noticed something. My confidence didn't budge. I found that *new* insecurities began to surface. I noticed some extra skin around my arms. More wrinkles also seemed to appear when I glanced at my reflection in the mirror each new morning. There were also new baby hairs, that appeared to be grey, sprouting up from my hairline.

What's up with that? I wasn't just seeing a smaller number on the scale, but a smaller bra-cup size came along with that. The thing is for years, I spent so much of my life nursing six babies. I did the math. I nursed my sweet babies for forty-two months altogether.

Hold your horses, I didn't nurse them until they were four. That's not what I mean. I mean the months compiled together. Months that I absolutely cherish. If you're a mom, you know how special and fleeting that time is.

Now let's rewind to the pre-baby era, my boobs were just fine. No complaints. I vaguely remember the days as a teenager where I didn't even wear a bra at times. What a time to be alive! Now today, if I did that, it would look as if I was smuggling deflated balloons from my kid's birthday party under my shirt! I jokingly tell my husband that I wish I had put back every dollar that we *would have* spent on formula over the years and I could have paid for breast reconstruction surgery by now. But I didn't. I spent that money saved on cute clothes for my babies. And diapers. Lots of snacks. Toys. Little League. Baseball gloves. Cheer uniforms. Groceries. Vacations. Snacks. Snacks. Snacks. More Snacks. Ice cream cones. Did I mention groceries? Or snacks? We have spent approximately $327,841 on snacks. I don't see myself ever being at a place to afford a breast lift and nip and tuck. Each time I get one kid out of braces, another one seems to have crooked teeth emerging and it's their turn to get their set.

However, if I would have, I'm sure that the very next month I would find something brand spanking new to be self-conscious about. The insecurities are as endless as the options of Dollar General stores in the south. But the good news is, God's grace is not a faucet that gets turned on and off. It's more like a river. Jesus didn't just say grace applies to everyone else; it applies to you too. Hebrews 4:16 says, "Let us approach God's throne of grace with confidence, so that we may receive mercy and find grace to help us in our time of need." Approach Him with confidence, friend, even if you have to fake it at first. His grace will cover you.

Here's what I want you to hear as you close this chapter: your purpose is not fragile. It doesn't disappear on the days you lose your patience, forget the permission slip, or serve cereal for dinner. It doesn't hinge on your productivity, your appearance, or your ability to keep it all together. Your purpose is steady and rooted because it was given by God, not earned by performance. And it shows up most clearly not when everything looks impressive—but when you keep loving, showing up, and staying faithful in the middle of the mess.

Motherhood will never look the same from one home to the next, and that's by design. God didn't mass-produce moms with identical gifts, personalities, or capacities. He handcrafted *you* for *your* children, for *this* season, with the wiring you have—Type Z and all. When you stop striving to be someone else and start walking fully in who God created you to be, something shifts. Comparison loosens its grip. Joy finds its way back in. And purpose stops feeling like something you're chasing and starts feeling like something you're already living.

So tonight, when the house is loud or quiet, clean or chaotic, I hope you'll pause and remind yourself of this truth: you are exactly where you are meant to be. The work you're doing matters more than you know. Heaven sees it. God sees *you*. And one faithful, ordinary, grace-filled day at a time, you are walking out your purpose—right in the middle of motherhood.

2021 – COVER PHOTO USED FOR MY PODCAST, FOR THE LOVE OF CHAOS

When a
mother prays,

HEAVEN LEANS IN.

Surrendering Your Burdens

I once cried over a teddy bear.

Hot tears streamed over my puffy, swollen cheeks and trickled down until they found their home, as a puddle formed on my big pregnant belly. The tears weren't because of the ever-growing stretch marks that covered every inch of my skin like a road map. A road map of the mountain roads that wound all the way from one end of my belly to the other. Not only was I nearly seven months pregnant with twins, I was also growing out of every last piece of clothing that I had. I was at the point in my pregnancy where I had finally resorted to my husband's wardrobe—oversized T-shirts with my belly peeking out of the bottom and large sweats. I know what you must be thinking, that alone is enough to make any first-time, young, expectant mom cry. Especially since the previous summer I had an assortment of bright colored bikinis. I knew deep down that I should probably just go on ahead and hold each of those a moment of silence and remembrance. Because, after this twin pregnancy, I would likely never be caught in another one again.

But the tears were for a totally different reason. As I gazed at the nursery my husband, my mom, and I had spent months, I felt a little silly as the tears couldn't stop. The little room was small. But it held a prayer we'd carried since we first built our house. This room once was used for storage, but from the beginning, we hoped and prayed that it would one day hold our first baby. Early on, I just never ever imagined it would have held two sweet babies at the same time.

One wall was pink; the opposite wall was blue. In between the two cribs held the most comfy chair I have ever sat in. I spent so many hours sitting there with my swollen feet propped up, dreaming of who they would be. What they would look like, what color hair they would have, and what their personalities would be like.

But on this particular afternoon, I was counting their teddy bears.

This was in 2010, the era before Amazon blew up and before shopping online became a normal thing. There were a lot fewer stuffed animal options for boys than there were for girls, might I add. Family and friends also had an easier time finding pink and frilly stuffed animals than they did finding the more boyish ones. To the naked eye, no one else would have hardly noticed a difference in the array of plush toys that was displayed at the head of each crib.

And that's when it happened.

I felt mom guilt for the very first time. A familiar emotion that would often rear its head regularly throughout my motherhood journey. This guilt was over teddy bears. And a fear deep down that I wouldn't be a good enough mom, because I had no clue what I was doing.

But honestly, who does? Also, under the teddy bears was a fear I didn't know just how to process aloud yet: What if I show a difference in my love?

During that first pregnancy I often wondered *how* I was going to love both of my twins the same. The immense fear that I would unknowingly and unintentionally, show a difference somehow. The irrational fear that I may possibly give one more attention weighed so heavy on my heart and mind. It felt like I was carrying an invisible backpack full of bricks around. Looking back, I realize that it's just something that happens when you grow life inside of you. And when my belly grew each time, with each additional pregnancy, my heart grew as well. I have no doubt that if I had twenty more children in this lifetime, I would have just as much love for them as I would all of my others. That's a no-brainer. But for someone that has never yet experienced motherhood, it was, what I considered, a logical worry. I thought I was crying over teddy bears, but I was really crying because I was worried I wouldn't be enough.

In spite of the fact that my sweet friend assured me that I would most definitely be begging anyone to take stuffed animals as the twins grew and accumulated more and more plush toys, I drove all the way to the mall (yes, malls were the happening place at that time) on a dreary winter evening that night in search of some stuffed animals for my little man.

As I arrived at the mall, I spotted the cutest little brown puppy dog that I paid entirely too much for. When I got back home to place it in the crib, all felt right in my world. Remember, I was a first-time mom. Looking back on that moment, I realize how small and silly that was. But it also serves as a reminder that mommas do everything in their power to make sure that their babies know that they are loved. Let me also pause and say that money and toys do not equal love. Even children know that.

My friend was right, eventually I was begging friends to take stuffed animals off my hands as we accumulated endless amounts of them throughout their first few years of life. I no longer cried over teddy bears. I no longer worried about not being enough. Because I knew God would supply enough love and grace for every season, with every child, every day.

If I Could Sit with My Younger Self

If I could hop in a time machine and walk back into that nursery, I would find my pregnant self and sit right next to her in that big comfy chair. I wouldn't scold her for crying; I'd just sit with her, give her a hug, and tell her a few things:

- You can do this—even when you feel like you can't. There will be days when you don't think you can, but I promise you that you can. Even when it feels overwhelming, you are stronger than you think.

- You aren't supposed to have it all figured out. Honey, listen, I still don't, even sixteen years later. But don't worry, you will master the art of winging it every day.
- Go ahead and get rid of every bikini that you own. You'll never be caught in one again, but you can rock a black one piece.
- You cannot pour from an empty cup. Take care of yourself too. Those babies need you to be healthy, both physically and mentally. Don't feel guilty for taking care of you too.
- Soak it all in; don't miss the magic because you're too focused on the to-do list. Though it sounds repetitive and cliche, it passes in an instant.
- You have a helper. The Holy Spirit is the best co-parent. He will give you the guidance, wisdom, grace, and provision to guide you every step of the way
- You have no idea just how much love and joy you have coming your way. And your heart? Don't worry about your heart. Loving them enough shouldn't be something you should worry about at all because God places that unfathomable love there the minute that you see those two pink lines. That love knows no bounds. It has no limits.

Not only did my love grow double in size that pregnancy, but it would expand exceptionally wide with each of my children that came after my first twins.

Surrender in Motherhood

A concept that I'll shamefully admit was hard for me at first was surrendering. Surrender means fully trusting and placing something into God's hands. Surrender for me looks like being able to pray over each sweet child and say, "Lord, Your will, not mine. Your plans for them, not mine. Whatever will You have for their lives, let it be. But Lord, please keep them safe. That's what I want most, for them to be safe."

When my middle son Dax was eight years old, he got very sick. High fever, body aches, headache, fatigue. I took him to the doctor, and he tested negative for flu, Covid, and strep. The doctor told me it was viral, and it would have to run its course. I knew in my bones that it was more than that. I took him back to the doctor almost daily for a week while desperately hoping for answers. But we got none. We were sent home as they assured us it was just a nasty virus. That week was definitely full of sleepless nights for us both. He was crying in pain, and I was crying, begging God to heal him. By Friday of that week, his fever was higher than ever. I went to get him out of bed and sheer panic came over me.

"Mommy, I can't walk." He was so lethargic he couldn't even lift his head up. In a moment that I wanted to panic completely, and scream, and cry, I held it together. I scooped him up, grabbed a bag and headed to Vanderbilt Children's Hospital. My mother drove us, and I remember the hour drive felt like days. When we arrived, they immediately were alarmed at his condition and wasted no time. They did blood work and imaging over his hip. They warned me that we could be looking at cancer. His infection levels were dangerously high, and a large area lit up over his bone. I had to go to the bathroom to have a breakdown by myself, where Dax couldn't see me.

Never have I ever felt more helpless as a mother than I did in that moment. The "what ifs" began to take over my mind. What if he has cancer? What if he gets sicker? Or worse what if he doesn't make it through this? I could feel the walls crumbling in around me in that tiny bathroom and felt as if I couldn't breathe. I began to pray some of my most desperate prayers, right in the middle of that closet-sized bathroom of that children's hospital. A few hours later, the doctors told us that Dax didn't have cancer, but he had a rare bone infection called Osteomyelitis. He required surgery immediately the next morning because his little body was septic.

Surgery is scary, it just is. Especially when it's surgery for your child. But I knew it was necessary. To make things worse, this was during Covid, so no visitors were allowed besides the ones who came with him to the ER, which were my mom and me. We were so thankful for an angel of a nurse who allowed his daddy to sneak in for a quick hug and prayer before Dax was wheeled back into the operating room.

When a mother prays, heaven leans in. We know when the battle is too much, so we go to battle in the spirit. We get on our knees until we reach the gates of Heaven. You see, it's those desperate moments that call for desperate prayers. Not the pretty, polished ones but the ones with the ugly tears and the trembling voice. I fully believe those prayers make hell nervous.

There are powerful prayers that come from a surrendered heart—when we come to the ends of ourselves and know that we have zero control over the outcomes or circumstances. But we are fully trusting in the only One who can heal, fix, and sustain us.

After a scary rollercoaster of weeks, our sweet Dax recovered. In fact, the doctors were completely amazed at just how fast he bounced back from surgery. You see, they had warned us that he would likely need multiple surgeries, and he could be looking at many weeks in the hospital. They sent a physical therapist to his room with a walker to teach him to walk again, but he didn't even need it. Because we serve a God who heals.

I know you've had those helpless moments too. Those desperate moments with desperate prayers.

Maybe you're gripping a diagnosis you weren't expecting.

Maybe you have a prodigal child that has gone astray.

Or perhaps you're battling a silent battle of depression and just want to feel like yourself again.

Surrender isn't me throwing in the towel because I don't care. It's me leaning not on my own understanding, but fully trusting God instead. And most days, in motherhood, surrender doesn't happen in an emergency room. Not all days look like a crisis. But surrender is just as important on those ordinary days as well.

The Weight We Carry

Last week, I ventured out to a softball tournament and grabbed my large "mom bag" on the way out the door. Even though I wasn't quite prepared for the day, I knew that my trusty bag held some sort of snacks and things we may need for the kids. As I made my way from the long stretch of steaming black top to find our spot at the quadplex, I felt as though I ran a marathon. Yes, it was hot. And yes, I'm a little bit out of shape. But this was different—my bag was so heavy it left a bit of an indention on my shoulder.

When I sat it down, I giggled a little at what I found inside.

There were about five half-empty water bottles, a can opener, a couple of odd pairs of shoes, several swim goggle masks, a couple outfits, sunglasses, sunscreen, and snacks. Lots of random snacks. My kids love to fish, so there was an entire can of whole kernel corn. So of course, that meant they must have a can opener to open their bait.

The point is this. This is how the enemy likes to hold us back and weigh us down. By carrying guilt or shame until our back hurts and we are sweating profusely from carrying the load. Until we have indentions on our shoulder from the weight of all of those things.

Sometimes we need to lay down that heavy bag and dump the contents at the feet of Jesus.

The clutter.

The mess.

The anxious thoughts.

The depression.

The disappointment.

The worry.

The guilt.

He can handle all of it.

He can trade all of those things for something way better.

Peace.

In Matthew 6:27 it says, "Can any one of you add a single hour to your life by worrying?" The Word is clear that we gain nothing from worrying, but I find myself doing it far too often. It's like a heavy dark cloud that follows us around in our everyday lives, but especially when it comes to our children.

Worrying that you're teaching them enough during the homeschool day.

Worrying about their hearts after their best friend turned on them.

Worrying about keeping them safe even when they aren't with you.

Worrying about the influences and the crowd they surround themselves with.

Worrying that they won't remember anything you've ever taught them about Jesus—or worse, worrying that they won't see enough of Jesus in you.

I've heard it said that worrying is like a rocking chair. Though it is constant movement in our minds; it gets us nowhere. There are so many things that we have no control of at all when it comes to our children, and that is scary for moms. I know it is for me. But each day, we have a choice to surrender it. Now, am I saying to ignore a mother's intuition or discernment? Absolutely not. Hold tightly to those, but let go of the rest, sister.

I'm also not insinuating that this is easy to do. Because I know this struggle firsthand. I'm encouraging you to protect your peace at all costs. Recognize when those worries and what ifs are fear-based. Worrying can be a stronghold that has a death grip on so many of us. But the only purpose it serves is to rob us of joy and peace. There is so much power in vulnerably saying that I may not trust people or situations, but I fully trust God. I may fear the unknown, but I trust that God is already there fighting every single battle on my family's behalf. He has shown me time after time again, so why would I question that He won't do it again?

When I feel those worries bubbling up to the surface, I've found that the only thing that brings me peace is to pray. That is, of course, *after* I come up with every possible worst-case scenario and voice every single irrational thought and fear in my mind. But then I remember that prayer is the only thing that *changes things*. A simple, ten-second prayer does more than all those sleepless nights. If you find yourself struggling with a heavy heart, pray a prayer like this:

Dear Lord, please give my mind and my heavy heart rest today. You know how much I love my children and I thank you so much for them, Father. You understand that unconditional love because it's how You love all of your children. And they are Yours before they are mine. Jesus, please help me to surrender all of my worries to You today. Your ways and Your plans are far better than mine. I also know that You are more than able to protect them and deliver them from any evil or harm. Would You guard their hearts and direct their paths? Lord, please keep Your hand upon them and Your arms wrapped around them and me today. In Your precious name I pray. Amen.

This is Not Forever

I found myself crying while signing a card for my little cousin's baby shower last month. I tried to describe to her briefly exactly what I would've told my younger self. But I couldn't choke back the tears as I thought about how fleeting seasons of motherhood were. If you're a momma, you know this all too well.

One minute you're rocking newborns, enamored by the heavenly scent of baby lotion and immersed in newborn cuddles, then, the next thing you know, you're watching them behind the wheel of a car while you have to pretend you aren't dying of a panic attack.

The phases may be different, but the purpose in each of them remains the same. From newborn nights where you barely sleep at all to toddler tantrums that wear you down and make you laugh; from pre-teen emotions when they're figuring out who they are to teenage independence when you have to learn to let go and slowly give them freedom even when it slowly breaks your heart—each feels like a new world every few years. I'm fairly certain with each also comes more raw nerves and gray hair as well. Each phase of childhood is equally important, and we should embrace the process of getting our kids to and from each of them. Sometimes in the thick of motherhood, we view those phases as getting from point A to point B and simply keeping our head above the water. But we get the privilege of loving and caring for these amazing little humans that God entrusted us with.

Even though the world where motherhood and childhood collide is amazing, and wonderful, and indescribable, it can also be the hardest thing in the world at times. But the hardest part isn't the chaos. I've become a master at managing the chaos. No, the hardest part is the weight of it all. The heavy parts that weigh us down as mothers.

Something we have to remember is the somber fact that this is not forever. That simple fact is enough to make me want to scoop my kids up out of their beds where they are sleeping and rock each of them while I cry my eyes out. My teenage son is six feet tall, but I think I could still manage it.

They won't always beg you to push them on the swing set for five more minutes.

They won't always ask you to brush through their tangles after their bathtime.

Soon enough they'll grow out of those cute footie pajamas that you have to wash every day because they're the ones they love most.

They won't always ask to snuggle up on the couch next to you. Those babies will grow. I've seen it with my own kids. That baby who I cried about not having enough teddy bears now towers over me. And his twin sister drives me to town now in her car. She texts me regularly and asks if we can go get coffee. Though this season with them is different, it's a beautiful one too.

So maybe surrender doesn't always look like a dramatic moment on your knees or a crisis that forces your hand. Maybe most of the time, surrender looks quieter than that. It looks like laying down the invisible weight you carry each day—the fears you don't say out loud, the guilt you replay at night, the pressure to be everything all at once. It's choosing again to trust God with what you cannot control and believing that He is strong enough to hold what you cannot. Surrender isn't the absence of love or effort; it's the deepest form of it.

And here's the beautiful truth that leads us forward: God doesn't wait for your life to be cleaned up before He steps in. He meets you right in the middle of the mess—right where the tears fall, the bags feel heavy, and the prayers feel unfinished. He uses the chaos, the uncertainty, the cracks, and the places you feel least equipped. God works *through* the mess instead of around it—and surrender isn't the end of your strength, but the very place where His power begins to shine.

FROM TOP LEFT TO BOTTOM RIGHT: APRIL 2010- WITH MY VERY FIRST, PRECIOUS TWINS, HUDSON AND PAISLEE; JANUARY 2014- WITH MY SWEET, CHUNKY BABY, DAX; JANUARY 2016- WITH MY SWEET, SECOND SET OF TWINS, COZI AND CUB; MAY 2020- WITH MY SWEET, YOUNGEST BABY GIRL, TILLIE

PART 2:

God Uses You Right in the Middle of the Mess

The pain is
not intended
TO DESTROY YOU,
but its purpose is
TO PURIFY YOU.

When the Wind Gets Knocked Out of Your Lungs

On the playground as a young girl, I remember falling from the monkey bars and getting the breath knocked out of me while playing one spring afternoon. If you know that feeling, it is scary and is a little difficult to describe. That feeling as though you cannot breathe. I remember on that specific day, trying to cry but I couldn't catch my breath to do so.

This happened to me again as a teenager while I was cheering at a ball game. I was a flyer and had fallen out of a rather high cheerleading stunt. I didn't see it coming, and even though I'd experienced it before, it was still terrifying.

Fifteen years later, that same familiar feeling found me. But this time, it wasn't physical cause, but an emotional one. And that feeling was far worse. This time, it took a lot longer to find my breath again.

It didn't happen on a playground.

Or at a football game.

But instead, within the walls of my home.

My life as I knew it collapsed before my eyes.

My husband, the only man I'd ever loved since I was fourteen years old, had been unfaithful. When I discovered this, it felt like my entire identity was under attack. Even now, many years later, I still struggle with talking about these events. Some days, it still feels fresh. I don't want the spotlight and heart of this chapter to be on my husband's failures, but I want to share my story of God's faithfulness through it all.

In a matter of minutes, my world and the picture of what I thought my life looked like collapsed to the ground, along with my physical body. The weight of my world crumbling down was far too heavy for my legs to hold. The cold bathroom floor was the closest I could get to how low I was feeling. Something about that cold tile was enough to bring me back to reality and let me know that I wasn't just experiencing a bad dream.

Immediately, I began to cry out to God the only way I knew how. Tears and groans from deep in my soul. Groans that I didn't even recognize as my own. The only word I could mutter was Jesus.

Jesus, Jesus, Jesus.

And that was enough. His name was more than enough.

Have you ever found yourself in a moment like that? A moment when you don't quite know how to pray or what to pray. All that you know is that you need Jesus in the most critical of ways.

I realized in those moments of desperation, when my world was flipped upside down, that I didn't have to come to God with lengthy, drawn-out, eloquent, polished prayer requests. He was already there. Right beside me, on the cold tile of the bathroom floor. He knew my pain before prayers even left my lips. He saw me in the most vulnerable state, and He met me right there.

Romans 8:26-27 says:

In the same way, the Spirit helps us in our weakness. We do not know what we ought to pray for, but the Spirit himself intercedes with wordless groans. And he who searches our hearts knows the mind of the spirit, because the spirit intercedes for God's people in accordance with the will of God.

Often, I wish I could go back to that night and give that young twenty-five-year-old "me" a tight hug. That young version of myself not only had the rug of security and joy in her marriage jerked out from under her, she was also coming out of a silent battle with postpartum depression. The weight of the world she knew and reality collided and the aftermath was hard to grasp.

Even now, eleven years later, I still struggle to write this chapter. I'll be honest, I selfishly wanted to leave this one out. I really wanted to have an authentic, funny, lighthearted book about Jesus and motherhood and all the moments in between. But here's the thing, we both know that isn't always how life goes. I skipped it, avoided it, and prayed about it, but ultimately, I wanted to follow the lead of the Holy Spirit. So I kept it.

I've often heard from pastors and ministry leaders that our greatest source of pain or struggle is where our greatest ministry and testimony lie. We just have to overcome the "but . . ."

BUT . . . it's painful.

BUT . . . it's embarrassing.

BUT . . . it's traumatic.

BUT . . . I can't go back to that place.

BUT . . . people will gossip about it.

BUT . . . people will judge.

And to those "buts," I say BUT . . . God. He is the one that will bring beauty from the ashes and use it all for the good.

Remember back at the beginning of this book when I said that "joy and sorrow can coexist." Well, I wrote that when I was thinking of times like these. Because even in the messiest of stories, just like mine—from my messy van to my messy testimony—God's mercy is greater. And the heart of this story isn't based on failure; it's about God's faithfulness.

I also wish I could say that was the only night I found myself in fetal position, lying on the floor, but unfortunately there were many. Too many to count, if I'm being transparent. This was a battle my husband and I fought for years. It's raw, vulnerable, and I'll admit, still painful for me to put into words. People often say "time heals all wounds." I've found that to be a lie. Time creates space, but Jesus is the only thing that can even begin to bring healing to those areas of our lives. I still wrestle with what happened and wish that I could rewrite parts of my story. But I realize that sometimes pain is part of the plan, part of our purpose. What the enemy uses to try and destroy you, God will work together for your good. Always. Even if we aren't sure how, He will. Life is a series of mountains, valleys, golden sunlit moments, and then moments of treacherous terrain. Even then, we have to keep walking forward. Even when we are battered, fatigued, bloody, and in the midst of the worst famine.

He is with You to Pick Up the Pieces

I'm reminded of a time when my youngest, most rambunctious son got a new Lego set for Christmas. This one had many pieces and was rather complicated, and a tad overwhelming even for an adult. My little Cub is so full of energy that without any effort he has the ability to slightly raise the blood pressure and heart rate for both of his grandmothers anytime he is around them. He thrives on adventure, danger, and testing his limits. If there was a modern-day Evel Knievel, it would be my boy. He's given his most creative efforts to assemble his own zipline out of rope and some wire coat hangers. I'm getting off topic, but I wanted to shine a light for just a moment on his adventurous little soul.

My boy was thrilled with his new shiny toy, and he was ready to get started on building it right away. You see, adventure may be his middle name, but patience most definitely isn't even in his vocabulary. So, I was surprised and impressed when he worked on this Lego set for three days. He built it, with the help of his daddy, for hours and hours until it was completed. My boy was so proud of the golden Avengers masterpiece he had created. He proudly displayed it on the dresser in his room. As we had family over the following week, he led them by the hand to see it.

A few mornings later, I heard a crash, followed by lots of tears. When I rushed to his room, thinking that I might find someone hurt, possibly from a homemade zipline, I was heartbroken by what I found. My sweet little boy, sitting on the floor with huge crocodile tears, as his Lego creation was shattered in tiny pieces all around him. I tried consoling him, but it did no good. Even if we did have the manual, there were pieces scattered everywhere, even to the corners of their messy bedroom filled with random shoes, scattered toys, and other Legos. I did the only thing I knew to do—I hugged him tightly and wiped away his tears. Then I started to gather the pieces and put them in a large zipper bag.

Isn't that just what our Jesus does for us sometimes? When we are on the floor, broken beyond repair. Shattered. We may be so broken that we can't even begin to sort out the pieces. But He comes along, wipes our tears, and begins to collect the pieces shattered all around us. He doesn't wait for us to pick up the pieces to approach Him. He wants us to simply surrender our brokenness to Him. His presence will be our peace in the midst of pain and heartache. Psalms 34:18 says, "The Lord will be close to the brokenhearted."

Though my seasons of heartache weren't due to any choices of my own, I still wouldn't rewrite any part of my story if given the chance. It was during those heart-wrenching moments when I learned my most valuable life lessons. I felt God closer than I had ever felt Him in my entire life and I learned to fully trust Him, even with my trust issues. I learned intimately *who I was* and *whose I was*.

He is with You in the Fire

While writing this chapter, I was reminded of a story in the book of Daniel that you likely heard as a child in Sunday school. The story of Shadrach, Meshach, and Abednego in the fiery furnace. They had refused to worship the golden statue that the King had commanded them to bow down and worship. Their boldness and bravery is something I remember being in awe of as a child while hearing this story. Here is another takeaway: obedience to God will cost you, but He will absolutely deliver you—just maybe not in the way you expect.

You see, God could have chosen to overtake the guards that threw His children among the scorching flames. He could have chosen to extinguish the fire all together, but instead He allowed them to walk through it. I love Shadrach, Meshach, and Abednego's response to the king in Daniel 3:16-17, "King Nebuchadnezzar, we do not need to defend ourselves before you in this matter. If we are thrown into the blazing furnace, the God we serve is able to deliver us from it, and He will deliver us from your majesty's hand." But y'all, the next verse is everything. In verse 18 they go on to say this, "*But even if He does not*, we want you to know, Your Majesty, that we will not serve your gods or worship the image of gold you have set up." That's faith. Knowing that God is more than able to deliver them, *but even if He does not, He's still good.* And choosing to trust Him either way, that's what faith is. Even when it's scary and even when it means death.

They were thrown into the fiery furnace, and in case the fire in itself wasn't hot enough, the heat was ordered to be turned up seven times hotter than usual. The flames were so hot, that it killed the soldiers that threw them in. But Shadrach, Meshach, and Abednego were all unharmed. When the King sent the guards to check on them, they were amazed at what they saw. Daniel 3:25 says, "Look! I see four men loose, walking in the midst of the fire; and they are not hurt, and the fourth is like the Son of God." This is the part where I give you permission to put down your coffee cup, stand to your feet, and shout, "Who was that fourth man?" He was our Jesus! Jesus showed up! The same One who is with *us* in the fire.

Here is something I need you to know, sister, something that I have seen for myself, through trials and fiery furnaces of my own. You and I, as Christians, as followers of Jesus, *are not exempt from the fiery furnace.* Just like God didn't extinguish the fire that Shadrach, Meshach, and Abednego walked through, He chooses to meet us and walk with us through it. He delivered them from *within* that fiery furnace. It doesn't mean they didn't feel the heat from the blazing flames. It does not mean that they didn't experience fear when they were tossed among the heat to die. They still had no choice but to walk *through* it. You see, sister, this is where your faith is tested, and this may be the very place where your *testimony* is born. It's within those flames that you are *refined*. Faith isn't tested when things are going smoothly and when everything is comfortable. Your faith is forged within the fire.

Daniel 3:27 says, "They saw the fire did not harm their bodies, nor was a hair on their heads scorched; their robes were not scorched, and there was no smell of fire on them." You see, when they got delivered out of that fire, they had a testimony that nobody else had. They had a story that was probably hard for others to believe. But it was true and people who didn't even worship Jesus witnessed the undeniable power of our Savior *through* them. Whatever fire you walk through, just know that you aren't alone. Jesus will be walking with you through it, and you're gonna come out the other side, with not even a hint of smoke on your clothes. There are lessons that the fire can teach you, that no mountain top moment can. The pain is not intended to destroy you, but its purpose is to purify you.

In November 2016, I watched in horror and heartbreak as the news showed one of my favorite places engulfed in flames. A devastating and unexpected forest fire had overtaken the beautiful landscapes of the Great Smoky Mountains National Park. It was gut wrenching to see a place I considered a "home away from home" experience such a catastrophic event. It's a place I visited multiple times a year since I was just a kid. Ironically, 2016 was also the very same year in which I found my own personal life up in flames for the very first time. The one I referenced earlier in this chapter.

About a week after the fire, my dad took my oldest son and went to help with relief efforts. Together, they passed out food, blankets, and prayers to all those many that were affected. I was able to join them shortly after, and although I had been up to date on all of the news coverage, seeing the devastation firsthand made the reality sink in. It looked like an apocalyptic scene from a movie. Cars turned upside down, endless piles of rubble, scorched and twisted remnants of what used to be homes and businesses. It was heartbreaking to see such a booming and beloved place, turned into a ghost town in a matter of days. The Gatlinburg we always knew and loved would likely never be the same again.

The following year, my family took a trip back to the Smokies. I love to hike and be in nature, and my soul was craving it. As we took a drive into the area, on the windy, narrow, mountain roads, I noticed something I didn't expect to see. Among the ash and the dead, scorched treetops, there was new growth.

And in case you didn't already know, God specializes in bringing beauty from our brokenness. I have a Bible cover that is torn and tattered and should probably be replaced but I love it too much to let it go. It says, "He makes beautiful things out of dust." I purchased this cover when I myself felt like mere dust—shattered beyond repair. But friend, He swept me up and held me close until I felt like myself again.

The heartache I experienced was a cycle due to a series of events over time. It wasn't until 2023 that I finally began to see a light at the end of that dark tunnel. For so long I had the battle of taking two steps forward in my healing journey and then I'd find myself taking five big steps back. A counselor that I did countless sessions with looked at me one day and said, "Do you want to be a victim to your circumstances? Or do you want to be victorious through them?"

At first, I wanted to reach over and slap him. Just a little. I clenched my shaking hands into a fist and thought to myself angrily, "How dare you?" How dare he ask me that when my life as I knew it was crumbling like an underbaked sugar cookie into crumbs on the ground. I craved justice just as I craved a juicy watermelon during pregnancy.

But guess what, friend? He wasn't wrong. And that thought-provoking statement made me do just what it was intended to do: think. I didn't want this to be a death sentence to my spiritual life. I could choose to walk away and choose to be a victim, because let's be real, I was a victim. Or I could choose to be victorious through Christ. I could allow Him to sweep up all the crumbling around me and create something new within me.

While writing this book, I almost prophetically proclaimed over my life that those days are over. I'm not going back. I'm not going back *unless* it's to go back and help rescue women that are in the same valleys I was once in. The valley of self-doubt, intense heartache, unforgiveness, trauma, depression, and anxiety. I want to stretch out an open arm and let those women know that they are not alone, even though they may feel that way.

You see, when life knocks the wind out of you, you learn to recognize the demeanor and posture of another sister who is gasping for spiritual air. I've had my heart broken enough that I can recognize it in someone else. There is a hollow ache that I once held in the same way in my own eyes. Even if a woman is still showing up to work, still sitting on the bleachers at every game to watch her babies play. Her big sunglasses can hide those even bigger dark circles from the sleepless and tearful nights. That quietness she carries is louder than thunder in a spring storm. Oftentimes, she avoids eye contact, and her body language shows her state of weariness and fatigue.

You see, I know that look and that demeanor because I have worn it well. And while doing so, the Holy Spirit has taught me how to recognize it in another sister. Call it discernment. Call it PTSD. Either way, when I see it, I don't judge or want to walk away. It makes me want to draw near.

To see her.

To try and reach her heart or at least offer a kind word.

To pause and remember when that *was me*.

When I see others hurting like I did, it makes me hurt.

One thing heartache teaches you too is empathy.

So that you can truly see people in a way like Christ does.

Like my friend going through an unwanted divorce.

And another friend's foster baby—after a year of loving and raising her—was unexpectedly placed back with her biological family.

Seeing a friend having no choice but to walk away from her marriage due to her husband's alcohol and substance abuse.

In Scripture, we see that Jesus never walked past the hurting and the wounded. He was never in a rush when it came to them. He stopped what He was doing to minister to them. I think of Jesus recognizing the hurting and hemorrhaging woman in the crowd who touched the hem of His garment. If I were with Him on that day, I would have likely been overstimulated by the crowd of people and the noise. But not Jesus. Jesus noticed her. The one who stepped out in faith, among the crowds, among her own shame and humiliation about her condition.

He is with You in the Aftermath

If you're holding this book in your hands right now, you've also experienced pain. Maybe not the kind of pain that I'm referring to, but pain, nonetheless. We all have. Physically, pain is your body's personal alarm system. It signals that something is damaged, wrong, or in danger. Similarly, emotional pain signals damage, whether loss, rejection, heartbreak, or brokenness. Emotional pain can't be seen, and unlike a physical injury or wound that heals over weeks or months, emotional pain lingers. It doesn't just ache in the body, it aches in the deepest parts of our souls.

During the particular night when the breath was knocked out of me (and many other nights that followed in the months and years after), I felt a deep ache in the center of my chest where my heart is. I couldn't quite explain it, but as I was in agonizing, emotional pain, it manifested in my physical body as well. It manifested for me in crazy ways: Chest pain, hair loss, shingles, weight loss, panic attacks, insomnia, and even sores on my scalp.

We all have pain that leaves scars on our souls. They are wrapped in moments of disappointments, both big and small. Moments that come along and flip our world upside down.

- The divorce
- The unexpected death
- The affair
- The secret addiction
- The bankruptcy
- The fire
- The diagnosis
- The depression
- The broken friendship

Never in my life have I cried out to God more than I have during these moments. Moments that I wish weren't engraved into my memory like a rusty knife. The moments on the bathroom floor—running water in my bathtub to drown out the sound of my wailing and grief-soaked tears. I look back now on those times and can hardly stand the regret I feel for rushing bedtime so many of those nights. Because no matter how much my own world seemed to stop spinning, life went on. And I was carrying the weight of the world for my babies on my shoulders. Trying to create a sense of normalcy and trying to keep them from knowing the depths of what was going on. Regretfully, I found myself watching the clock so many nights counting down for when I could say goodnight prayers, tuck them into bed, and go hide behind my bedroom door. It was only then that I could allow myself to grieve.

I remember admitting this guilt to my counselor at that time. I felt robbed of so much. My normalcy, my joy, my laughter that was usually always present, my patience, my energy. A verse that I found so much comfort in during that time was Joel 2:25, "I will restore to you the years that the locusts have eaten."

Something I have to remind myself of is that we have to allow ourselves space during those moments. Space to heal. Space to process. Space to rest. As hard as it may be to accept and see beyond the fog of heartache and grief. There is still purpose in the pain and there is purpose in the healing too.

My youngest son is quite a rambunctious child. He is also the only one of our six children that has accumulated multiple broken bones in his ten short years of life. Many of our family photos have him sporting a colorful cast of some sort.

You see, a broken bone needs rest, and it cannot be rushed. If you try to take the cast off too soon, it will delay healing or even possibly cause the injury to worsen. Our pediatric orthopedic doctor once made the choice to keep our son, Cub, in his cast for a little longer. Wise choice on his part. From the date of injury to his cast removal was nearly twelve weeks. The doctors were concerned that if he got the cast off too soon, he would reinjure it shortly after if it wasn't healed enough. The same goes for us. God will, no doubt, heal us completely, but sometimes that healing takes time, just as it does with a broken bone.

Here's the difference in a broken bone as a child versus a broken heart as an adult. One injury is visible, and the other one is not. The cast is a universal sign to others that it should be protected and handled with care. But when our heart breaks and it seems impossible to keep moving forward, the world doesn't even pause for us. It doesn't even try to slow down.

But friend, you have to rest. You cannot run at a breakneck pace while healing.

Sometimes after going through hard seasons, your body, mind, and soul are left drained. Sometimes we do need to take a break from people, social media, and our normal routines. Give yourself space to heal. It is hard to heal and recover from heartache or trauma when we run at a breakneck pace. It is ok to say no to certain people or obligations when your soul is recovering. When an athlete gets an injury, they don't continue running and practicing. They know that if they do this, the injury could result in permanent damage. I've often heard the quote "The comeback is often greater than the setback." But that comeback doesn't happen if you don't heal properly.

The same goes for your spirit. When your spirit or your heart is broken, it's so important to allow yourself time and space to heal. Seek out a good Christian counselor. Talk to a trusted friend. Get extra sleep. Eat your favorite foods. Set boundaries with people when necessary to protect your fragile spirit. God will absolutely send you the right people at the right time to intercede and pray for you.

One of my most favorite verses to cling to is in James 1:2-4, "Consider it pure joy, my brothers and sisters, whenever you face trials of many kinds, because you know that the testing of your faith produces perseverance. Let perseverance finish its work so that you may be mature and complete, not lacking anything."

When we find ourselves walking through the unexpected and the unimaginable, we still refuse to slow down. It's like the rug gets jerked out from under us and we find ourselves abruptly, and painfully, lying on the floor. Then we often go into survival mode. We aren't focused on being present because we are focused on just simply putting one foot in front of the other one. We do this all while juggling dinners, laundry, playtime, diapers, dishes, work, and all the other everyday tasks.

I first learned what a panic attack truly is in this season. I had more during that season that I've ever had in my life. I had to be put on anxiety medication just to sleep, because I would lay down and feel them coming on. If you've ever had a panic attack, you know how terrible and hopeless they make you feel. But the one thing you're supposed to do is focus on breathing.

He Helps You Catch Your Breath

In the book of Exodus, God reveals His name to Moses as YHWH.

Scholars and Rabbis have noted that in order to pronounce this, without vowels, it sounds just like breathing in and breathing out: Yahweh. To say it correctly, you don't use your tongue or your lips. Just breathe. Take a second and close your eyes. Now breathe in deeply. Now exhale. Breathe in. Breathe out. You've just spoken the name of God. Yahweh.

A baby's first cry, even without words, speaks the very name of our Creator.

A mother's deepest sigh when we are troubled and heavy hearted, calls out the name of God, without even muttering a word.

When your heart is shattered and all you have is a shaky inhale on the bathroom floor between endless tears, it reaches all of heaven.

When the wind is knocked out of you . . . Yahweh.

You're calling on the name of God as you breathe in and out, even in your moments when it's hard to breathe at all. Because God is never offended by your lack of words or eloquence—He meets you in your desperation.

Romans 8 says that the Spirit intercedes for us through "wordless groans." That alone means that He doesn't just answer polished prayers. He meets us in the mess, on the floor, when we don't even have the words. He hears every cry and He most certainly hears His name. Jesus, Jesus, Jesus.

This is a moment in this book that I wish that I could pull up a chair and sit with you, friend. I need you to know as you read this that I'm so sorry for whatever you have walked through that has knocked the wind out of you. You didn't deserve that. That pain you've felt down in the deepest parts of your soul. The kind of pain that still echoes, even if years have passed by. Even if you have suffered silently. God saw it.

I know that feeling all too well, and unfortunately, I myself have walked through many moments feeling like the breath was knocked out of my lungs. But here is what I want you to cling to, God isn't just standing in the doorway waiting for you to find the composure and strength to get up; He meets with you and sits with you exactly where you're at.

If you're in a season of barely surviving, if you're functioning on the outside, but unraveling on the inside, I want to tell you what I've learned the hard way too many times, sister. The pain may be loud, but Jesus is close to the brokenhearted. The fire and flames may feel intense, but there is a fourth man in there with you. The wind may have gotten knocked out of you, but it doesn't get the final word. Jesus will breathe life back into you again even if it takes time.

One day you'll see that God didn't just bring you through all of it, but He built something deep within the deepest crevices of your soul through it all, and it gave you an incredible testimony to help other women.

Because that's what Jesus does best.

He notices the hurting.

He stops for the bleeding.

He stays with the broken.

He brings purpose from all the pain.

So if all you do today is breathe, remember you're doing better than you realize. He will breathe new life into you, your marriage, and every single detail of your life if you let Him. Just keep breathing.

MAY 2023 – AT OUR VOW RENEWAL ON THE BEACH IN FLORIDA.
IT WAS A WONDERFUL DAY!

Jesus was misunderstood, but he **NEVER ONCE** misunderstood his assignment

When Flight or Fight Kicks In

Let's talk about the "nevers" for a minute. Have you ever found yourself judging someone else and found yourself saying, "I would never do that." "I would never handle a situation like that."

I can answer this one. I did this pretty terribly before becoming a parent. I look back now and laugh over just how ridiculous some of my "never" statements were. These all came around the ripe ole wise age of nineteen or twenty. Might I add, all of these never statements were muttered before actually having kids of my own. Let's go ahead and shake our heads, laugh together, and roll our eyes as you read this ridiculous list below:

- I'd never let my kids wear character-themed shoes or clothing (It was tacky).
- I'd never let my toddler continue to have a pacifier.
- I'd stick to a strict sleep schedule, and my kids would never sleep in my bed.
- I'd never drive a minivan, like ever.

In case you're wondering, I did, in fact, do all of the above. Now, six kids later, I find myself letting them pick out their own clothing most days. They have apparently forgotten critical skills like matching clothing, especially since becoming homeschooled. No doubt that my younger self would cringe at their choices. Just last week, I saw my twelve-year-old run out the door with athletic pants and a plaid shirt he typically wears to church. His younger brother tagged along right out the door behind him wearing a pair of Nike slides on a day that happened to be forty degrees. He did wear socks though, so that was a win. My mother briefly watched them while I had to take the kids to the orthodontist, and she was in utter shock and disbelief when she saw him in that attire. She's come to expect this with grandparenting six children, especially with me as their mother. With each kid, I have let a lot of stuff go. As long as they're happy and fed, that's a win for me. Wardrobe worries went out the window a few kids earlier.

And yes, honey, they did in fact wear many pairs of light-up shoes, lots of characters, and I never once batted an eye. My middle child was addicted to multiple pacifiers until he was four. He also went through a streaking stage where the only accessory he had while running around the house were three to four pacifiers with the little stuffed animals attached to them.

Oh, and the sleep schedule? After the first two kids, sleep training went completely out the window. Wherever the kids would lay and fall asleep is where they end up. I literally chose not to care. Because let's be honest, sleep is sleep. It also becomes a rare luxury when you have a whole lot of kids. I often describe our bedtime routine like a game of whack-a-mole. Once I get one child laid down, another one pops up out of nowhere. As I'm writing this book, we currently have seven kids including our sweet exchange son. So this game of whack-a-mole right at bedtime can drag on for hours. One will need a drink of water. The next one will want me to tuck them in, yet again. After that, my curious one will want to talk about the book of Revelation.

Oh, and the minivan thing? I just want to take the time to publicly apologize to every single momma that I judged for driving one. I know I judged hard, but karma bit me even harder. I get it now. And we can all laugh together because I now drive the mothership of all vans. A twelve-passenger one to be exact. And I love it. Friends, I can put an entire wagon in the back without even folding it down! I may have taken out a few hundred curbs in the past six years that I've driven it, but it is my favorite thing. I love my big van. My twenty-year-old self would be curled up in a ball crying somewhere if she saw her future self cruising in that big thing.

We live, we learn, we grow, life hits us, it humbles us, and at times, it knocks us to the ground. The point of all of that is this: sometimes, boldly and pridefully stating "I will never" can be a dangerous statement. Whether it be something as lighthearted as your children's wardrobe or as heavy as a separation or divorce.

After the wind got knocked out of me emotionally, I thought about running away. With my kids, of course. All six of them. To somewhere warm and sunny. But then again, Alaska also sounded enticing. Not because of the Northern Lights or the gorgeous snow. The single most persuasive factor about Alaska was the fact that it was 3,000 miles away from home. 3,000 miles away from my small little town with big-time gossip. Gossip that oozed like an infected wound and spread everywhere it landed. I wanted, with all my heart, to be as far away from there as I could get.

You see, isolation wasn't the desire—escape from the gossip, judgment, and pain was. My deepest pain had been put on public display, and the rumor mill was working overtime. Never in my life had I felt more shame, humiliation, and heartache.

But can I tell you a secret? A lot of the rumors were true. Exaggerated? Probably. But mostly, unfortunately, devastatingly true.

I found myself teetering between chatter of reality and rumors and the effects were becoming detrimental to my soul. People I thought I could trust pulled away while others completely betrayed me in ways I could have never imagined. And the ones that didn't pull away, I put the distance between us all on my own. I did the pulling and tugging until I isolated myself even more. I was in my own form of emotional solitary confinement, and I gripped the key tightly in my hands. I was too hurt and humiliated to even attempt to vent to anyone. There were no words that I could find to justify my decision to stay. I knew they might judge or question my antics, because I was also doing a whole awful lot of that all on my own.

Underneath the weight of the judgment and opinions of it all, I found myself buried and couldn't seem to find a way out. I felt exposed in a way I'd never quite experienced before. Far worse than those familiar nightmares where you find yourself out in public without any clothes. I was a victim of the gossip and the public display of pain, and I felt so incredibly humiliated. The enemy loves using people's words to bruise a woman's identity. But it wasn't just my image that was bruised, it was my spirit. I wouldn't really say bruised—I would say beaten and battered, then dragged through the mud.

Fight, Flight, and the Fear Beneath It

Are you familiar with the term "fight-or-flight?"

Fight-or-flight is an instinctive, well-known stress response to a threatening situation. It prompts you to stay and fight or run and flee from danger. It's kind of like your body's built-in alarm system. God actually designed it to protect us from danger. When your brain perceives a threat, it signals your nervous system to either:

- **Fight Back** → argue, push back, defend, prove yourself, or legit throw hands.
- **Flight** → escape, hide under the covers, withdraw, want to disappear or move away.

Here's the thing, your brain cannot always tell the difference between a physical threat and an emotional one. So sometimes your body reacts the same way to intense gossip, slander, rejection, betrayal, and heartbreak as it would if a massive bear was chasing you. That is why you feel like you could have a heart attack any moment. That is why your thoughts spiral, and that's most certainly why you get defensive. That is why you shut down. And it is why you want to escape 3,000 miles away from wherever you are.

Your body believes it is protecting you. Feeling the urge to respond in fight-or-flight does not mean you are weak, it means you are human. And something I have learned about this response is this; it is rooted in fear. I know I can speak for myself when I tell you that I have stayed in that state at times for far too long. When that happens, it robs you of moments that you should find joy in. But you can't relax because you forgot what it feels like to be emotionally safe. It's not that I chose to feel this way; it's that I simply didn't know how to get out of that state. Fight-or-flight was like a guest that overstayed its welcome. Before you know it, you find yourself entertaining it far longer than you'd like. You're out of guest towels and patience, and you are ready for this unwelcome guest to hit the road.

Support Systems

During this time that I wanted to escape life, isolation became my companion. Which was unfortunate, because as isolated as I felt on the inside, it was also smack dab in the middle of the holiday season. I was forced to press on. I dreaded going anywhere, especially the grocery store. I simply wanted to disappear. To Alaska, perhaps. I imagined I would have to get past my fear of flying, and I'd have to start packing some warm clothes for the journey. I most certainly couldn't tell my parents because they would talk me out of it and put a halt to my plans. Though they are my biggest supporters, they would utter the words of how ridiculous that idea was, and although they would be right, that's the very last thing I wanted to hear.

I knew I could tell my sister-in-law, and she would help find a way, because she is adventurous and supports even my dumbest ideas. She also is a secret keeper. She has seen me in my worst moments and still cheered me on to the finish line even when it wasn't a good idea. In spite of all of that, I knew, subconsciously, that no matter how many miles I traveled I could not escape my problems or the mess I found myself in. No matter how much I wish that I could. A new zip code has no power to heal an old or a fresh wound. Not to mention the fact that I have no sense of direction. I also lose my phone sometimes, while I am talking to it. 3,000 miles away seemed like a great idea, until those little humbling nuggets of truth surfaced to the top of my clouded thinking.

Not to mention the fact that the enemy would have an absolute hay day if he could get me to run away. To flee from my home and my support system. Because they were there too. But Satan wanted me to have tunnel vision and only see the people that made me want to run away in the first place. I had friends and family that checked on me, day in and out.

Sometimes in life we have to cut ties, set boundaries, and deny access to people we thought we'd do life with forever. Although those times are painful, and oftentimes unexpected, God sends reinforcements. Not crowds. Not flocks. Sometimes just a faithful few.

The ones who checked in when I got quiet.

The ones who defend my name in rooms I'm not in.

The ones who sit with me to make the silence a little more comfortable.

The ones that don't flinch at the tears.

The ones that show up and take the kids for a fun weekend trip, without even being asked.

The ones who boldly proclaimed victory over my family when I could barely see a sliver of hope.

When the enemy wanted to isolate and push me to want to run to Alaska, God sent those reinforcements right to the doorsteps of my home. With prayers. With casseroles. With pizza for my kids. With hope. With encouragement. With so much love.

Together my village—my small but mighty village—my family, and a few amazing friends reflected the heart of Christ. My gratitude for those that walked through it with me can't be described in words.

And in those moments I wanted to switch zip codes or run 1,000 miles away with my kids, I'm incredibly grateful that God, in His kindness and mercy, surrounded me with people who refused to let me walk alone.

Satan knew he couldn't cancel the assignments God had given me, but he would love to send me on a detour, the long way around. He would love nothing more than to delay, distract, and derail the plans and blessings that God had in store for me. Satan cannot change the calling on your life, but he can absolutely confuse your direction through fear, lies, anxiety, comparison, betrayal, and heartache. And before you know it, he will get in your head and talk you into fleeing from the very place God wants you to stay planted.

I imagine some of you being there right now, just like I was.

Maybe you're carrying secrets you've been afraid of sharing your whole life. The pain, regret, and trauma are too much at times. The option of disappearing or running away seems easier than the vulnerability of confessing pain or shame from your past. You feel like if you speak up, you'll be ripping off old scabs that never really healed. Or worse, you'll feel like no one will understand you.

Maybe you're the strong one. The one who always shows up. You're steady and constant in all the right ways to your friends and to your family. You're the one who always stands in the gaps and checks in on everyone else. You pray so fervently and seem so confident in your faith, that no one notices when you, yourself are struggling. Strength becomes a costume that seems impossible to take off. You feel like you're running on empty.

Maybe it was betrayal from someone you love. When trust is broken, it also breaks your heart in a way that is hard to describe. Now your senses are always heightened and you can't fully be at peace, because you're always looking over your shoulder just waiting for someone to stab you in the back. You want so badly, with everything in you, to protect yourself. But in attempting to do that, you only end up building really high walls that are nearly impossible to knock down.

Perhaps, you're the happy one. Everyone fully depends on you to give them a good belly laugh. Your personality radiates and you have a way of finding joy and laughter in even the worst of situations. But life isn't feeling very funny right now. You feel like you have to put on a happy face, but every smile is draining life out of you. You feel like there is a heavy dark cloud following you around that isn't visible to anyone but you.

You could be in a similar situation that I was in. Maybe you've become the central topic of your own town's rumor mill. You hear the whispers at the grocery store and the beauty salon and you want nothing more than to escape the stares and gossip. You want so badly for others to know the truth, so that somehow, they might understand you or sympathize with you.

We've all found ourselves in similar situations, but oftentimes we fear talking about our struggles with other women. In times when we feel isolated, we can always turn to our God who understands our pain.

God Knows Heartbreak

It is absolute truth what the Bible tells us in Psalms 34:18, "The Lord is close to the brokenhearted and saves those who are crushed in spirit." No matter what kind of mess we find ourselves in or what happens in life to bring us to our knees, He is already there. And when the pain is too deep to even explain or comprehend, His peace overwhelms and surpasses all of our own understanding.

During these erratic escape plans I had in my head, I would talk to God. Even though isolation was my companion, Jesus was my right-hand man.

I struggled to vent much at all to others, but I didn't hold back when it came to God. He was the only one who had a front-row seat to the train wreck that my life had become. While others had broken my heart, God was putting it back together, even though it took time.

On one specific day, I broke. I broke differently than I did in the days prior. I broke down to Jesus. His response to me was a reminder that He is always listening. Through my ugly tears, I muttered the words that I barely got out between sobs, "I don't know anyone that knows this kind of pain this kind of betrayal; there isn't even a book I can read! I don't know anyone that has experienced this degree and this level of betrayal."

In the quiet, I heard His still, small voice.

"Oh, but you do. It was me."

It was me.

Those three words stopped me completely in my tracks. They also broke me and humbled me. He also told me that there isn't a book, because I would be the one to write it. That my testimony would bring comfort to others.

I fell to my knees and cried out to him for the millionth time that day but this time with a fresh perspective. When He said, "It was me," it was like a lightbulb went off in my brain. Everything changed.

Something shifted in me that day. I can't quite explain it. I struggle with the words to describe it even now as I write this chapter. I do know one thing, it was pretty supernatural. It was a deliverance in a sense. Trust me, I've seen deliverance. I was raised up Pentecostal from the time I was a baby and broke my teeth on a tambourine. I believe that the gifts of the spirit are still alive and well today. In fact, I plan to write an entire book on these things one day. I know in my soul that God can deliver you in an instant from certain things, while other things take much longer.

But we can take comfort in this: Jesus knew pain. He certainly knew betrayal. Even with His closest friends.

Peter denied even knowing Him.

Judas sold Him out for a few pieces of silver.

Because even though He was our Savior, He was human too. Jesus Himself had been front and center in the rumor mill in a way that none of us will ever comprehend. He endured mockery, accusations, and betrayal—yet He never allowed any of that to define Him.

Now, I know I've already said this once in this chapter, but it's so important that I want to say it again.

Jesus is close to the brokenhearted.

Jesus was also misunderstood, yet He never once misunderstood His assignment.

I think of Him in the Garden of Gethsemane the night before He was crucified. He was so overwhelmed with sorrow and stress that He sweated drops of blood. He cried out to God to ask Him to take this cup from Him, to remove the suffering. But ultimately, He submitted, saying, "not as I will, but as you will."

He knew His pain was for a much bigger purpose.

You know what? Perhaps, yours is too.

He was lied about, misjudged, accused, rejected, gossiped about, hated. But in spite of all of that, He never once lost His identity. He didn't shrink back to make them more comfortable. He also didn't defend Himself to every voice. He simply was planted firm in who His Father said He was. You see, He didn't hightail it to Alaska to escape the pain. He stayed planted and trusted His Father with it. That's most likely the most perfect model of surrender He displayed for us. Staying the course and clinging to the cross to follow God's will for Him and all of humanity.

Surrender everything. Every hurt, every ounce of bitterness, every sliver of control. Lay it all down at His feet. He can handle our mess. Something beautiful happens when we unclench our fists and completely surrender smack dab in the middle of our suffering. It does not mean you're giving up. It isn't a white flag of some sort. It's simply choosing to place what you cannot fix or carry into the hands of the only One who can. Now, sister, this is not a one-time thing; this is a daily decision to lay it all at His feet.

Whose Voice Will You Listen To?

I know it is hard if you yourself are in a similar situation. This is a time I wish I could take off my shoes and sit next to you on a comfy couch, over a warm cup of coffee. We could cry together. I could even bring a punching bag if that would help release some frustration. We could even find a deserted road in the middle of nowhere and smash some plates. Whatever works. But in all seriousness, if we were to sit face to face, I'd want to encourage you to ask yourself some tough questions.

- What is God trying to reveal to me in this season?
- How can I use this as an opportunity to grow my faith?
- How can I find purpose in this gut-wrenching pain?

Whispers, meaningless gossip, and opinions used to shatter me to my core, but that specific day, God delivered me from it.

Your pain may have shaped you, but it does not shift who you are in Christ. It doesn't own you either. And other people's opinions? Though they may be hard to swallow and they may get stuck in your throat like a spoonful of peanut butter, they don't really matter.

Does it mean it doesn't hurt?

No.

Does it mean it doesn't still affect you at times?

Absolutely not.

It just means that your identity can't be found in what others whisper about you. Your identity can only be found in what God says about you.

There comes a time in every woman's life when she has to choose which voice she decides to lean into. And sister, I know, firsthand, what a struggle that can be.

The crowds?

The critics?

The gossip?

The ones who spun a false narrative to deflect the role that they played in your pain?

The ones who whispered and pointed?

Or the quiet, gentle, unmistakable voice of our perfect Father?

You see, all those voices may be loud, but it's just noise.

His voice is final and frankly, it's the only one that matters.

The moment I stopped trying to perfect my image in the eyes of people, I finally had room to step fully into God's purpose in my life.

Pleasing people serves no purpose.

Power struggles have no purpose.

Chasing perfection has no purpose.

Purpose requires surrendering.

Purpose requires boldness.

Purpose requires being ok with rejection.

Purpose becomes possible when we stop pursuing others' approval and we pursue God instead.

Jesus Will Meet You Where You Are

Sister, I want you to walk out of this chapter feeling a little freer.

Not because everyone understands you, but because the One who formed you does. This is the chapter you stop running from all the noise and begin to run towards the only voice that counts.

Here's the thing, I know if I ran away to Alaska, my pain would have followed me there. My suitcase would have been weighed down with heartache, anxiety, and humiliation. None of that would have stayed in Kentucky. I may have escaped my hometown, along with the rumor mill, but my problems would have accompanied me there. And along with them, most likely a bad case of frostbite. During my experience, I saw that God doesn't always relocate you when He restores you.

I think of all the stories in the Bible where He reveals the same sentiment.

- Elijah hid in the cave out of fear, he felt depressed, tapped out, and suicidal. But God met him there.
- Jonah ran and we all know how that turned out for him. He found himself in the belly of a whale. And God met him there.
- Moses fled to the wilderness and God appeared to him in a burning bush there and ordered him to return to where he ran from.

God doesn't always relocate us in order to restore us.

We cannot hide from God. We also can't outrun our testimony. If you feel the urge to flee, to disappear, to hide under the covers, or to start over in a land far away—I want to lovingly share with you this. You don't have to run to be restored. You just have to invite Jesus to meet you right where you are. God will put you together right in front of the people that tore you down. You just have to trust Him.

Your healing won't come from running away, friend. It will come from you staying, surrendering, and allowing Jesus to meet you in the very place you wanted to escape.

I thought Alaska was the answer. I was wrong. Turns out, Jesus was. The same Jesus who was with me in my mess is with you in yours. The Jesus who whispered "It was me" in my deepest pain is whispering "I'm with you" in yours. And sister, that very place is where your purpose lies.

Community
isn't something
we wait for;

IT'S SOMETHING WE BUILD.

When the Table's Not Big Enough

As I sat at a table in a crowded, beautifully decorated conference room, I received a text. I knew it would be from my best friend that would be arriving shortly to join me. She and I were alike in many ways. Both our driving skills and sense of direction—or more honestly, lack thereof—happened to be a couple of things we had in common. So, I was assuming she might need directions on how to get to the event space.

I was anxious for her arrival. She'd moved to another state, so we typically only saw one another a few times a year. This conference and trip to North Carolina was something we'd both been looking forward to. A girl's trip that we were actually going to follow through on. It was also a chance to catch up and have a real conversation without our kids interrupting us. When I entered the conference room, I felt bold because although I knew no one, I knew I'd shortly be joined by my friend. So, I grabbed a seat up front since I'd arrived early. I happened to be seated directly in front of Lysa TerKeurst herself. Just the woman I had come to listen to.

You see, this writer's conference was something that had been on my heart for years. Every year, I would get the emails, swoon over the list of compelling speakers, and make every excuse not to attend. I was a mom of six, so that was my number one excuse. Many of the years that I wished to go I was either pregnant, nursing, or knee deep in toddler tantrums. But this was my year. I snagged my ticket months before, booked the hotel in advance, and arrived early. Likely the first event that I was early for in my whole life.

You should also know this . . . I'm scared of flying. I don't know what happened to me once I became a mother, but I became a bit of a weenie when it came to heights and planes. Before kids, I had flown multiple times. Florida, Texas, NYC—no problemo. I even enjoyed the rush of taking off and landing. But after I had my first set of twins, we had the opportunity to fly out to be on The Steve Harvey Show in Chicago. I had three kids at the time—my twins were four and my baby was eight months. I had a panic attack on the plane and swore I'd never ever do it again. I kissed the ground once I got off and held tightly to that promise. To this day, I have yet to get on another plane. Despite my husband and parents begging me to fly to Charlotte for the conference, I insisted that I'd drive seven hours by myself. My mother cried for weeks. I know that sounds like I'm being overly dramatic, but I assure you that I'm not. My parents worry about me, even in my thirties. In their eyes, I'm still a teenage girl, despite me having six kids of my own. All they could see was the dangers of me traveling on the interstate several states away. But it made them feel better because they knew I would be meeting up with my friend, so we'd be together once I arrived in Charlotte.

I woke up at 3:00 am to make it to Charlotte in time for the first day of the conference. I could hardly wait to arrive and learn from the best of the best all about writing and speaking. I was also excited to try some new restaurants with my bestie in this town we'd never been to. As the lights lowered, I checked my text notifications and my heart sank.

She wasn't coming. Something had come up that was out of her control and there was also an issue with her ticket. Either way, she wouldn't be my plus one like we'd planned. All of my excitement and anticipation for the weekend I'd waited so long for turned into intense disappointment and slight nausea. My confidence that I had when I first entered the large conference room suddenly diminished, and I felt myself sinking into my seat. Tears that were welling up in my eyes began to sting, and I felt a rather large lump in my throat as I did my best to choke back the tears. I wanted to cry. But I didn't want to cry. Because the only thing more pathetic than sitting at a table without a friend at thirty-six years old would be crying at that very same table. I looked around and noticed everyone around me seemed to be talking. Everyone seemed to have someone but me. The chatter and laughter sounded muffled, because all I knew was this: Now, I would be spending three days all alone in an unfamiliar city, with unfamiliar faces.

Disappointment and Rejection

Had *I known* I would have been traveling to a large city by myself and staying in a hotel by myself, I would've just stayed home. But, after pouting for a bit, I realized maybe, just maybe that was the whole point of me not knowing. Sometimes if we know the whole picture ahead of time, we will let fear of the unknown become deeply rooted in our hearts and minds. I know that I do. And if we aren't careful, we let fear of the unknown cloud our vision so that it's hard to see the blessing that's right in front of us.

I wanted to ask God, "Couldn't You make this part of the itinerary? Couldn't You have given me a heads up before I drove all this way?"

But I had a strange sense of peace that came over me. It was like God was saying, "Chill, I've got this."

In the conference Facebook group, an online community where attendees would chat and share info, I noticed that there were several women planning a meetup for dinner and invited anyone to join them. I pumped myself up to step out of my comfort zone and go with them. They all seemed friendly and approachable, and they also had some cute headshots. They were pretty, professional, and they looked like they most definitely had their lives together. I would totally love to be friends with them. I commented excitedly as I saw the details of the dinner place they were meeting at; it happened to be the same one that I was hoping to try while in town. Perfect! Maybe this was all part of the plan! A few moments later, the woman who was organizing the dinner responded, "Sorry, our reservation is full."

I was late to the game. It had already filled up. It was like salt in the wound. Ouch. Rejection sucks. It just does. Even if it's unintentional. It may feel like a quick sting, but for someone highly sensitive to it from past trauma, it can easily trigger a full-blown nervous system meltdown. Your heart races, skin feels tight, you find it hard to get a good breath. Panic sprints from your head to your toes.

If we aren't careful, we can sit with this feeling too long until we begin to believe these things about ourselves. I sat there staring at my phone while the enemy started painting a false narrative in my mind:

See? You don't belong here after all. You're awkward. You're unorganized. You certainly can't get your life together enough to write a book either. You're late. You're the outsider. Those women have business cards and headshots. You have anxiety and an old applesauce pouch in the bottom of your purse. Go back to your room. Hide. Call it a night. You tried. Or better yet, pack up your suitcase and go back home to Kentucky.

Rejection can make us feel a lot of things, and none of them feel good:

- Sadness
- Shame
- Worthlessness
- Unwanted
- Embarrassed
- Too much
- Not enough

And frankly, that's exactly all the things that the enemy wanted me to feel. He wanted stings of rejection to shove me into isolation. He wanted it to seep over every corner of my soul until I did what I always tend to do when I'm hurting. Retreat. Crawl back to my little cave in my hotel room. Maybe even build a blanket fort of self-pity. If he could distract me with disappointment, I might miss the lesson that God was trying to teach me that afternoon.

Because let's be real, that's one of Satan's oldest tricks in his book: *Rejection → Isolation.* If he could get me alone, he could get me in my own head with spiraling thoughts and lies straight from the enemy.

In case I wasn't wallowing in self-pity enough before, I most certainly was now after that response. I immediately felt like I was in seventh grade, and no one wanted me to sit at their lunch table. That was the moment I thought about ordering pizza and going to my room early. I would likely spend my night wallowing in even more self-pity and eating an entire pizza all by myself.

That's when I felt God begin to speak into the situation. Sometimes His voice in our lives is loud, other times it is not. But you'll know it's God by the nature of the message. The voice of God brings peace and offers reassurance. In this moment, He wanted me to rebuke all the words and negative emotions the enemy was trying to magnify. Jesus was giving me an invitation. To partner with Him to discover my purpose for being there. God, in His goodness and kindness, was simply positioning me. It wasn't a punishment; it was a pivot.

A moment later, I had a light bulb moment. I'd just arrange my own dinner with strangers. Before I could talk my fingers out of posting, I did it. I arranged my own dinner. Anyone was welcome. "If anyone wants to come, let me know! Comment below! I'd love to make some new friends and network as well!"

Anxious thoughts raced through my mind. Did I look desperate? Would they know this was my Hail Mary attempt at some sort of connection with other women who might be in the same boat as me? To assume that maybe some were also at a conference with no friends? What if no one showed up, and I ended up sitting by myself again?

I said a prayer and asked God to work it out.

He knew my heart.

He knew my worries.

He also knew that my favorite plans were cancelled plans. So He already knew that I was getting cold feet the minute after I posted that. Pizza sounded nice. I'd get some extra garlic sauce and maybe even some hot wings. My comfort zone sounded *even nicer*. Maybe I'll just hit delete on that post. I could veg out on some junk food and binge watch something on Netflix—maybe cry a little. It sounded like a plan.

I had left my phone number on the post, and I immediately began to get texts and comments. I called the restaurant and reluctantly made the reservation. By the grace of God, I navigated through downtown Charlotte without taking out any curbs or bicyclists, until I finally arrived at the trendy restaurant. I parked on the street out front and sat in my car for a moment. I let out a deep sigh and contemplated pulling out quickly and nonchalantly—the local Papa John's was on speed dial.

But I didn't.

I stepped out and went inside. The host showed me to the table. I sat at the end and ordered my regular—a tall glass of water on the rocks with extra lemon. The table seemed to stretch and grow each time I awkwardly looked up from my phone. As I sat there being the only occupant for our reservation, I began to contemplate my most recent and sporadic life choices.

What was I thinking? Arranging dinner in a new city? What if I am left here at this long table by myself all alone? How pathetic am I? Why did I even come to this conference? I should have just streamed it online like I had done in the past.

But before I could feed any more negative thoughts, I began to feed my starving self that was still hungry from all the travel that day. And here's the thing, no matter how stressed or depressed I am, I will never turn away chips and salsa . . . or chips and guac . . . or chips and queso. Like ever. If I ever do, you know that I've really hit rock bottom. Just as I began to crunch through my emotions on crunchy chips and as I drowned my sorrows in cold salsa, women began to arrive. One by one, then two by two.

They were all so kind and we all hit it off right away. One woman encouraged me so much on my journey to write this book and shared her own experience of a book she had just recently written. She was so humble about her success, and it encouraged me so much. There is something special about breaking bread with strangers. Or in our case, we shared our hearts over shared baskets of chips and queso. I knew during that dinner that this was God's plan all along. Our dinner table became so full that they had to pull up extra chairs. You see, none of us came to the table with perfect words or polished stories. They each chose to show up and bring it all to the table that night. Their vulnerability, maybe even a little awkwardness that comes when first meeting complete strangers, their open hearts. Somehow, the queso must have helped each of them with courage. Tears began to fall as I heard each testimony from each one of the women. Testimonies about heartbreak, loss, insecurities, fear, shame, illnesses, overcoming addiction, forgiveness, and so many more. Every testimony pointed back to how God brought them to this event. Many of them had been to this event before, but for many, like me, it was their first time. The Holy Spirit had set a fire in each of their hearts and souls for ministry. Whether it was through nonprofits, podcasts, writing books, speaking at events, Christian influencing, or writing blogs. I knew through every heart that was poured out and through all the tears that fell, that God was right there in the midst of that long table, with baskets of chips and salsa.

He had orchestrated all of this. Every last detail. Every woman who was brought to the table. Every story. Every connection. When we walked out of the restaurant that night, I felt like I had thirty new sisters. It was hard to believe we were all just strangers a couple of hours prior. As I headed out, I noticed the table that I had missed out on, the reservation that was full. And that's when it hit me.

In life, if there isn't a seat for you, build your own table and make room for more.

Building a Bigger Table

And honestly, I think that's why God didn't just give me a lesson; He gave me a picture. Both through that night at the restaurant and in a vision. You see, months prior, during a prayer walk, the Holy Spirit placed a beautiful picture in my mind. It was vivid and colorful, and I wish, so badly that I could describe it in words. But even more so, I wish that I could paint the picture to show you. But my lack of artistic abilities would likely leave you confused and laughing if I tried. Your girl here cannot draw a stick person, much less a beautifully detailed intricate painting of what I saw in my spirit.

It was a long, overflowing table. Picture in your mind the famous painting of The Last Supper. I was sitting at a very long table similar to that. The table held the most beautiful spread of dishes. Plates, saucers, teacups, the whole shebang. There was a beautiful spread of pastries and colorful food. But here's the thing that stood out the most: Nothing was the same. Nothing was matchy. It was quite the opposite, actually. It wasn't curated. It wasn't color-coordinated. It wasn't Pinterest-perfect. It was mismatched dishes—a chipped plate beside mason jars and a piece of nice vintage China. We were all in different chairs too, none were the same. There were place settings that did not match in the least, but they belonged there anyway. And there I was, shoulder to shoulder with women. All different kinds. Different ages and phases of life. Different stories, different scars, different personalities, different backgrounds. We seemed to be in sync with one another, in some way though.

As I saw this during my prayer walk, both sweat and tears were streaming down my face as I saw the beauty of what God was revealing to me. In a gentle whisper I hear, "I'm preparing a table for you, and it looks like this." That's when it hit me that this is what God envisions for His daughters. Not polished. Not performing. Not perfection. Not an Instagram-worthy setup. Just a place to gather together for one purpose. It was messy, unique, a bit chaotic, but it was so beautiful. It was held together perfectly by His grace. I realized in that moment, that we didn't need matching hearts—just willing hearts that beat the same. For Jesus.

Community isn't something we wait for; it's something we build. So sister, if you've been waiting to get your life together, you'll be waiting the rest of your life. We all come with flaws, scars, and loads of baggage and laundry. Maybe you're hesitant for other reasons. Because you've had lots of moments where the reservation you wanted was full.

Maybe your "reservation is full" moment looked like this:

- Being left out of the group text
- A friendship that has drifted
- Seeing pictures and reels from an event you weren't invited to
- The email that says, "Sorry, we've decided to go in another direction."
- The broken relationship
- The effort that isn't reciprocated

We've all had those moments as women. If we aren't careful, they'll hold us back in hesitation. The enemy loves to take a bad moment and paint the narrative in a way that makes you feel lonely, rejected, and left behind. When you feel him doing this in your own life, jerk that paintbrush out of his hand and pop him in the head with it, sis. He doesn't get to paint the picture, you do with God's steady hand and guidance.

Building the table can look like this:

- Send a text. Reach out first. Plan dinner
- Be a safe space—be the friend that you need in your own life
- Be intentional—show up even when you're busy
- Offer support—pray with other women, connect through your testimony
- Be willing to serve God through serving people—take a casserole when they're sick. Send a text to encourage them. Small acts of kindness go a long way.

- Don't overcomplicate it—just be obedient to the women God is calling you to reach.

God has a way of working all things together for His good. I walked into the conference that following morning with a different, fresher perspective. A clearer heart and steadier mind. Not because my feelings magically disappeared overnight, but because God had shown up for me like He had time and time before. He replaced lies from the enemy with peace and His truth. I wasn't alone. I wasn't rejected. In fact, many women were also in my shoes. Some had traveled all the way across the country by themselves. The next day at the conference, some of those ladies at the other table, that I had missed out on, were seated with me, and I made connections with them as well. I saw smiling, inviting faces all around me that day, and until the end of the conference.

Better Plans

I was beginning to see the bigger picture. God had a divine purpose for my wrecked plans. His plans are always better. It reminded me of Ruth in the Bible.

Talk about wrecked plans. If anyone understood wrecked plans, it was her. You see, Ruth didn't plan on losing her husband. I'm sure it wasn't in her five-year plan to lose her home either. She didn't have plans of starting over in life. Who really ever does? I'm also fairly certain it was never in her itinerary to follow her mother-in-law seventy-five miles on foot, through rugged terrain. *I mean, I love my mother-in-law dearly, but I'm not sure either of us love one another enough to tackle that kind of adventure together.* Ruth had the option to go back home. To her comfort zone. To what she knew. To familiar faces. But she chose another route. The more difficult one. She didn't allow any of those tragedies or her own grief to have the final say in her life. She walked into Bethlehem as a "foreigner" which meant "outsider" in biblical times. That wasn't her normal stomping grounds. It wasn't her home. She was the "new girl" with no connections. And in the face of adversity and the unknown, she trusted God to take care of her in her next season of life. Instead of throwing in the towel and going back home, she was brave, humble, and stayed the course. Not only did God honor Ruth's faith, loyalty, and obedience to Him and her family, He intricately placed people in her path to bless her along the way. God didn't just give Ruth a pep talk. He gave her provision. He gave her people. He gave her purpose.

The truth is, when you really think about it, we've all had a Ruth season in life as women. We've all had moments when we've contemplated turning back. We've all had moments when we've wondered as we trembled in fear "what's next?" We've had to start over after the loss. Maybe it was the loss of a parent or spouse. The silence and grief that came from a miscarriage or infertility. At some point, we felt like an outsider. Maybe it was a move to a new town, having to start over from scratch. Perhaps you've had to come to terms with a life you would've never chosen for yourself after an affair or an unwanted divorce. Maybe your finances are a wreck, and you worry how the bills are going to get paid at the end of the month. You may have found yourself having to take on a humbling second job that you weren't expecting or planning for at this phase of life. Maybe you're gripping at a difficult diagnosis for your child. And you're struggling coming to terms with the fact that their childhood isn't panning out like you planned. Instead of playdates, you find yourself at appointments for them. You're in a state of exhaustion like never before as you are a caretaker and an advocate at the same time.

Sister, if you're reading this with a lump in your throat, because you're currently in one of those seasons, I want to sit with you for a minute. If I could, right now, I'd give you a big bear hug. Please know that this last paragraph was led entirely by the Holy Spirit. I've prayed while writing this and asked God to show me you. I've paused and I've cried. I cry as I type these words, because He did. He showed me you. You, the one who is reading this book right now. I may not see you physically, but please hear this:

God sees you. He sees you. I promise you that He does. And He loves you. He loves you so much. You may have been surprised by these things, but God was not. He knows the whole story even when you may struggle with the chapter you're currently living in. It's not the whole story. You see, God has a way of redeeming stories. I know He has in my own life. He will in yours too, friend.

If you find your own plans getting dismantled and you struggle to see what's ahead, remember RUTH.

R – Recognize the voice

Ask yourself: Is this thought placing shame and rejection on me? Does it make me panic or want to flee? If the answer is yes, then it's not the voice of God. And sister, that's the only voice you need to allow in your life. God's voice is steady and comforting but also convicting at times. His voice is peaceful and offers you hope. Listen to that one.

U – Use what you have

Sometimes we have to go to plan B when plan A gets derailed. The goal is not to stay stuck, but to keep moving forward. Use your phone to text a friend and ask for prayer. Use your resources. Find another restaurant. Make your own dinner reservation. Start a Bible study. Arrange dinner with a friend and pray together. Use your feet. Go for a hike. God pours into me so much when I hike. So many ideas for this book you are reading took place on prayer walks I did last summer. Move your feet and watch God move in your life. Just don't go back to the cave.

T – Take the next step

It doesn't have to be a big one. Just a step. God isn't looking for you to have it all figured out. He just wants your obedience. Show up, even if you feel awkward. Speak up, even if your voice is shaky. Do the scary stuff. I promise God will meet you there when you do.

H – Hand it over to God

This means releasing control. Surrendering. Decipher what you can control versus what you can't. I'm old-school and I like to make lists. I have countless notebooks with random notes and lists. I even utilize the backs of receipts and old envelopes. When you can physically see things in a list form that you can control, focus on that.

What you can control:

- Your next step
- Thoughts you allow to take root in your mind
- Your effort
- Your boundaries
- Your routines
- Your attitude

What you cannot control:

- Closed doors or rejection
- Other people's opinions
- Being included by someone else
- Outcomes
- Your past

Obedience doesn't always look loud or flashy. Sometimes it's mundane and ordinary. When we are faithful in our field God will always bring the harvest.

God doesn't always show me the whole plan because He's more committed to my trust than my comfort. Sometimes the missing details aren't punishment—they're protection. You see if God would have revealed to me that my best friend wouldn't be at the conference that weekend, I would have bailed. He hid that detail to push me out of my comfort zone. Sometimes He leaves out the details to protect me from my own panic.

God graciously displayed to me the importance of community. But at the same time, He also taught me that it cannot be a crutch. As humans, we naturally seek validation from others. We crave connection with people. But it cannot become our main source of life and fulfillment. I have to be ok with walking into a room alone. Sitting alone. Driving to a conference alone. Because I know God is with me.

I can't stop thinking about that picture the Lord showed me of the table—the long table, the mismatched dishes, the wide variety of chairs that didn't quite match but they belonged there anyway. God was prophesying to me what He was about to do in that specific experience in this book and in the lives of the women who read it. So if the plans change unexpectedly, or if the reservation is full, don't retreat. Show up anyway. Build the table and always make room. God will surely show you His beautiful blessings when you do.

JULY 2025 - ANDI AT THE SHE SPEAKS CONFERENCE IN CHARLOTTE, NORTH CAROLINA

He doesn't
expect you to
GUARD IT PERFECTLY;
He expects you to
GUARD IT PURPOSEFULLY.

When the Window is Open

"But if a watchman sees the enemy coming and doesn't sound the alarm to warn the people, he is responsible for their captivity. They will die in their sins, but I will hold the watchman responsible for their deaths." – Ezekiel 33:6

A few nights ago, I complained for the hundredth time this season that our bedroom was cold. Every other place in our home was well-insulated and warm during this cold snap we'd been having. I slept with socks and extra blankets and couldn't quite understand *why* our bedroom felt like it was perched on the outskirts of Antarctica. The following day, as I was packing in groceries, I saw it: the smallest crack in our window. My husband had gone through our bedroom window to plug up an extension cord and forgotten to close and lock it afterwards. It was hard to notice from the inside, because it was such a tiny opening.

You could hardly see it, but you could most certainly feel it. The smallest of cracks can change a room. All it takes is the tiniest of gaps, barely visible to the naked eye and suddenly the atmosphere shifts.

This reminded me of the schemes of the enemy. Because most of the time, the enemy isn't marching up to your front door. He isn't coming with a megaphone to announce his arrival. He likely isn't knocking hard on the door, waiting for us to allow him inside. If he did, we'd all be ready to fight. We'd be prepared. We'd be aware of his arrival.

No, he's quieter than that.

He's strategic, momma. He looks for the windows we've left cracked. Not purposefully. Not because we aren't good mommas. Not because we aren't good Christians. Not because we don't wholeheartedly love Jesus. It's because we are tired. We are overwhelmed and overworked. Our schedules are overloaded and we are stretched thin. We are trying to balance it all without falling completely off the beam. We're trying to get our kids to all their activities. Trying to keep all of our many children alive and fed. We are trying to serve at church. We're doing our best to remember to thaw the meat out for our dinner each night. We're breaking up fights among our kids while also trying to remind them they're a child of God, not a UFC fighter. We're busy searching for the missing shoe and the socks that seem to disappear each and every morning. We are trying to make time to wash our hair and drink enough water each day. This list could go on for days. I don't have to tell you how busy you are; you already know that all too well.

Windows are subtle. Sometimes you don't even notice the small cracks until you feel a shift in the atmosphere. It may be small enough to ignore, but big enough to let something in. Like my cold draft that filled the room that I slept in.

The enemy doesn't need an invitation—he just needs access. This is why it's so important that we recognize any windows or access points that could allow the enemy to infiltrate our homes.

Before I go any further, I want you to know that I have felt such an urgency to expose the enemy so that you can be aware of his schemes. But I also want you to stand boldly on this truth before we go any further in this chapter. The same power that raised Jesus from the grave *lives in you.*

An Awakening

My heart raced, panic sending shivers down my spine. We were sitting at a long table—Cody, the kids, and me—eating dinner together as a family. It was familiar. Safe. Or at least it should have been. Outside, complete darkness pressed against the many windows surrounding us.

Everyone else was relaxed. Talking. Laughing. Actually getting along for once. A rare miracle, right up there with finding matching socks in our laundry baskets. Normally, dinner is loud and chaotic. Someone's chewing too loudly. Someone's throwing food. Kids argue over forks, over turns to talk, over who's talking more. It's messy. It's chaotic. And somehow, it's my favorite.

But this dinner was different.

I was standing at the end of the table, tense, alert—like a watchman in the night. Like a sheepdog guarding its flock under a moonless sky. I didn't know what I was waiting for, only that something felt wrong.

Then I saw them. Headlights pierced through the darkness like a spear. A dark car with windows too tinted to see inside began circling the room—slowly, deliberately—like a drive-thru around my family. No one else noticed. Just me.

Slow.

Silent.

Strategic.

Like a shark circling its prey.

That's how the enemy works. He waits. He watches. He strikes when we're distracted—when we're tired. And the most vulnerable are always the easiest targets.

The windows started opening.

One by one.

I ran to slam them shut, but as soon as one closed, another opened. It felt like a sick game of whack-a-mole. I was sweating, panicked, racing around the table while my family laughed and ate, completely unaware.

Then the car stopped. A hand reached through an open window—grabbing for my children.

I fought with everything in me. Exhausted. Desperate. Refusing to give in. These were the babies I carried. And I would fight every demon in hell before I let them touch my children.

A sound jolted me awake. I sat straight up in bed, drenched in sweat, heart pounding. It felt like waking from a childhood nightmare—but I knew this was different. I ran through the house checking every window, every lock.

And then I knew.

The windows weren't physical.

This wasn't an ordinary dream.

This was a warning.

An awakening.

I've always had vivid dreams. But years ago, God began giving me dreams and visions that carried weight—messages from the Holy Spirit. Not often. But unmistakable.

I know some of this may sound uncomfortable or even triggering. Faith has been mishandled by the church before. Spiritual language has been weaponized. Skepticism makes sense. But Scripture urges us to be watchful. There is a real enemy. And his goal is simple: to steal, kill, and destroy. He wants unbelief to keep you numb. He isn't just distracting you—he's aiming to devour.

But hear this clearly: he is already defeated. The battle was won at the cross. Still, until his time is up, he wants collateral damage. And mama, he isn't just coming for you. He's coming for your marriage. For your home. For your children.

That night, I grabbed my anointing oil and walked the halls of my home. I prayed over doorways, walls, and bed frames. My prayers were desperate—but awake. Not routine. Not rushed. *My faith was steady, but it wasn't urgent. I was incredibly faithful, but I was also incredibly fatigued.* My faith hadn't been weak; it had been tired. There's a difference.

A mother in survival mode isn't spiritually fragile—she's stretched thin. These are the very seasons when the enemy grows bold—circling quietly, just waiting for exhaustion to dull our discernment. Quietly circling. Looking for access points. That's what the dream was about. Not locks. Not windows. Access. The places we've left unguarded because we're exhausted. The cracks we've normalized. The areas we've been too tired to tend to.

But awareness changes everything. And that night, I woke up. But even in our exhaustion, we have to stay aware. Vigilant. Consistent.

In biblical times, anointing oil was used much more often than it is used now. I grew up in a background that fully embraced the use of oil, prayer cloths, and laying hands on people for prayer. It wasn't until 2022, when I had a real encounter with demonic forces at a church camp, that made me fully utilize my oil. I anointed my kids so much that week that they told me their lunches at church camp tasted like straight-up oil with traces of cinnamon bark.

Going back to biblical days, the oil had cleansing and sanctifying properties. It was used then just like now, as an act of symbolism. To represent that that person or thing that you're anointing is set apart and belongs to the Lord. Anointing oil is any kind of olive oil that has been prayed over. It doesn't have to be fancy or expensive because it really isn't even about the oil itself, but what and who it represents.

As I was anointing every surface of my home, I began to pray for a hedge of protection over my family. Over each baby. I say baby, but at this time I also had young teenagers as well. But as any momma knows, our babies are always just that: our babies. No matter the age, the phase, or the fact that they tower over us when they give us hugs. We still see them as ours to protect—always.

But the longer I stood there in the darkness—heart pounding, oily hands, sweaty hair, checking every sleeping child and every squeaky lock—the more that I was reminded of something. The dream was not about latches and locks; it was about access. It was about entry points.

Identifying Open Windows in Our Homes and Lives

The enemy doesn't always announce himself loudly. Or boldly. He waits patiently. Finding the perfect moment to slip in through the cracks of whatever we've left unattended. Through areas that we've normalized. Through what we've been too exhausted to guard. Let's look at a list of common areas of access.

Movies and Music

This is a big one. And a controversial one, might I add. Have you ever heard the song "Be careful little eyes what you see? Be careful little ears what you hear?" Well, that may have been designed with children in mind, but those commands are ones that we can all apply to our lives at any age. As the watchmen of our homes, we have to be cautious about what we are allowing on the screens that play in our homes.

Several Halloweens ago, my middle son demanded that I turn off a seemingly harmless movie because he said it was demonic. I giggled at first, but then I felt incredibly convicted as a parent. If my eight-year-old has sharper discernment and convictions than me, *that was a problem.* I began to pray for God to open my eyes and sharpen my discernment in this area, and He did. With each year, I become more alert and aware of what we allow.

I know this is a topic not everyone embraces or agrees with. On social media, so many influencers post disclaimers that state "For entertainment purposes only." I get the skepticism. But here's a thought-provoking question: What are we entertaining? And for what purpose?

A couple of years ago, I was watching an interview with actors and cast/crew from a show that I loved as an older teenager/young adult. It was about vampires and witches. The directors recalled witches from New Orleans calling them and letting them know that their show was "playing with fire." She went on to say that they were warning her of the danger and threat she was bringing into every living room across

America with this hit show. The actors were reciting real, actual spells in each episode. That's not just entertainment. That's witchcraft. That's darkness. And light cannot come into agreement with darkness by allowing that within the walls of our homes and casually dressing it in the form of entertainment.

Unforgiveness and Bitterness

This one is a tough topic. At least it is for me. At some point, a very *hard point* in my adult life, I was living under the assumption that forgiving someone was letting them off the hook for what they did. But if we look closely at Scripture, it's very clear where Jesus stood on the topic of forgiveness. Even while on the cross, being brutally beaten and crucified, He cried out for His Father to forgive His persecutors. Forgiveness isn't optional. It's necessary. When we choose not to be obedient to that command, we are unintentionally giving the enemy a foothold into our lives. If we aren't careful, he will begin to plant seeds of bitterness into every crevice of our hearts.

Before we go any further I want to sit with you on this for a minute. Please don't slam the book shut at this point, because I know just how hard this is to do. To be honest, this has been convicting me as I write this out. For years, I thought something was wrong with me, because I couldn't honestly and fully forgive. Something really helpful that I learned through this season is that forgiveness isn't always a one-time event. Sometimes you have to forgive daily. Every time you're triggered. Each time you remember. Every time we feel that sick feeling in the pit of our stomach. It doesn't mean the person we forgive is off the hook or that they won't face consequences for how they hurt you. It doesn't mean that they won't one day stand before a just God and have to answer for how they mishandled you. It just means that *you* are no longer held hostage by holding onto it. It's willingly placing them in the hands of a *just Savior* so that you can walk in peace.

Unconfessed or Willful Sin

This doesn't mean we have to live perfectly. The only One who ever walked this earth that was perfect, was Jesus Himself. Can I be transparent for a second? I have a confession to make. In my younger years, I viewed God as sitting on a throne just watching and waiting for me to mess up. I wish so badly I could go back and convince myself in my teenage/young adult years that I had it all wrong. I knew God was good all the time. I loved Him. But my relationship with Him was very fear based due to a spirit of religion. Once I truly experienced the love of God I could see His grace much more clearly. He wasn't placing shame on me when I messed up. He was placing conviction on my heart because *He loved me.*

Romans 3:23 says, "For all have sinned and fall short of the glory of God." *Not some, but all.* If God expected perfection out of us, He never would have sent His Son to die on the cross for our sins. But He knew without His blood, we would never stand a chance.

Unconfessed sin is kind of like living with a smoke alarm going off and deciding the problem isn't the noise. It's feeling like we don't need to repent. That we can handle it on our own. That we can live life by our own rules. Rules that we bend and break or toss out completely.

Willful sin is a little different than struggling. Struggling says, "I hate this." Willful sin says, "I'll keep this, and I'll just ask forgiveness later." The difference here is the heart posture. And in my humble opinion, willful sin is dangerous territory. The more that we get comfortable in our sin, sometimes our heart becomes hardened and calloused, making conviction harder to reach. God's grace is abundant and it is given freely, but we cannot abuse it. Willful sin could look like a variety of things:

- Ongoing dishonesty
- Sexual sin
- Anger outbursts/lack of self-control
- Bitterness you refuse to release to God
- Substances you use to escape

- Harsh and uncontrolled speech that you've normalized
- Constant gossip

I tell my kids all the time that conviction doesn't feel good, but it's a good sign. It's a sign that you have the Holy Spirit with you. It's God's way of drawing us back into Him through His love and grace, not condemnation. We cannot cling to our comfort and conviction at the same time.

Occult Objects

Ouija boards, crystals, tarot cards—these objects listed are more obvious ones. But there is another area that falls into this category that is sneakier: new age practices. You see, with new-age practices, many people that start out dabbling in it with mostly pure intentions. But they are unknowingly inviting dark *entities into their homes and lives.* Let me say that again. They invite in dark entities, *not light, like new-age tries to disguise itself as.* You simply cannot dress the devil up in a nice angelic gown and somehow call it pure. Any practice that includes prayer and promotes peace and pathways that do not come from God is a dangerous and dark counterfeit. The enemy is the author of lies and confusion and he has infiltrated every detail of this topic through and through. He must be called out and called down. The only source of power, peace, and prayer should come through Jesus Christ.

Idolatry: This is anything that we place before our relationship with God. I'll go first. One that I've struggled with is one that is in my hands a large portion of the day—a cell phone. I can't tell you how often I have started my day by checking my notifications, emails, and social media before my feet even hit the floor. Not to mention these are also huge distractions in many different aspects. This is something that I wholeheartedly believe is a struggle for many. Productivity has also become an idol—we put tasks and agendas before time with God. We have to learn to be still and spend time with Jesus, even when it's hard to slow down.

Discernment Disarms the Enemy

Discernment is everything. It's simple and steady. When you feel a shift in the atmosphere, use what I call the 3 Ds of Discernment:

- **Detect**: "Something feels off."
- **Discern**: "Holy Spirit, is this fear based or a nudge from you?"
- **Disarm**: "In the mighty name of Jesus, I shut this window. I refuse to come into agreement with lies, fear, bitterness, evil, deception, or distraction."

Don't overcomplicate it. Start small. Ask God to reveal to you one window that is open in your own home in your own family. I promise you when you pray specifically about this, He will begin to reveal things to you. The Holy Spirit gives discernment to us as a gift.

To fight these battles, we must know the word and walk in the authority of the Holy Spirit. Before we can worry about our children and husbands, we must first check our own hearts and come into alignment with Christ. A prayer I regularly pray when talking with God is one that David cried out in Psalms 51:10, "Lord, create in me a pure heart."

I fall short daily, I just do. No matter how many times I try to get it all right, I get something wrong along the way. But repentance is the acknowledgement of that. It's surrendering it to God and asking for forgiveness and praying for a fresh mind and heart daily. A pure heart is essential when dealing with spiritual warfare. Please take note *that I didn't say* a perfect heart but a pure heart. A heart filled with God's love and truth can crush the head of any spiritual and demonic strongholds. Luke 10:19 says, "Behold, I have given you authority to tread on serpents and scorpions and over all the power of the enemy; nothing will hurt you."

Sister, this chapter was not intended to entice fear. Instead, its purpose was to ignite a boldness deep within your soul. My hope and intent in writing this wasn't meant to make you afraid, but to make you aware. God chose you for such a time as this. To be a protector, a mother, a wife, a watchman over your flock. But He doesn't expect you to guard it perfectly; He expects you to guard it purposefully. One window at a time. One small choice at a time. One prayer at a time. I know God gave me that dream to not only have my own eyes opened, but to help open yours as well, friend.

Tonight, you're not likely going to have a dark-tinted car circle your home. But when it does, you'll be ready. Ready to close any windows. Ready to make the enemy wish he'd never messed with you or yours. Because a praying momma, paired with God, who knows the enemy's schemes, is a powerhouse. And God created you for this very assignment.

The longer I've walked with Jesus, the more I know this to be true.

JOY ISN'T A FEELING; IT'S A CHOICE.

Joy is a fruit of the spirit — not a personality trait.

Finding Joy in the Messes, She Laughs

I have a confession to make. This is a safe space, and I feel like we are at a point in this book where I can say this to you. Sometimes I laugh at funerals. Not because I think any part of a funeral is funny but because I have some kind of disorder that has plagued me for as long as I can remember. As a matter of fact, one day, hopefully far, far away when someone stands to give my eulogy, I hope that they start off by saying, "If she were here right now, y'all know there is a very good chance that she would be in a corner giggling."

For as long as I can remember, I have laughed. Over everything. It has been an emotional outlet of sorts. This is the thing about my laughter: it also shows up in terrible timing with zero respect for social cues. For all of my life, it has been both a blessing and a curse, an awkward trait that embarrassed me for years, but eventually revealed something important about Jesus, joy, and survival.

And just so you can visualize, this isn't the cute little giggle where you can politely cover it with your hand over your mouth. This is the kind that erupts the moment I try to conceal it. We're talking full-blown, shoulder-shaking, tear-evoking, at times nearly pee yourself, unequivocally, 100% noticeable, and unfortunately, a lot of times, inappropriate scenarios. It shows up like an unexpected guest that doesn't even knock, just barges through the door.

Serious conversation?

I laugh.

Doctor telling me something important? Or even worse, while I was pregnant and he dared to mention a vagina or worse s-e-x? It was like I immediately reverted to a middle school girl. I would giggle.

My child does something that they shouldn't do and needs strict parenting structure over?

I laugh.

I've been this way forever. My parents survived it, but I've most certainly put them in some awkward situations over the years. My husband would also tell you we've had some close calls with altercations because of it. Because laughter at the wrong time can be a recipe for a disaster or a recipe for a butt-whooping.

Honestly, if there were to be a spiritual gift for awkward laughter, even in the worst of moments, I'd most definitely be walking in my calling every day of the week. Part of it is how I'm wired, part of it is probably nerves, part of it maybe delirium from the chaos of parenting six kids. However, you want to spin it, you can come up with your own assumption. I bet as you're reading this someone else may have come to mind that does the exact same thing. It may even be you.

I know what you must be thinking. Why am I reading a book written by this unhinged woman of God? I get it, but hear me out, sis. Here's the twist: I used to feel guilty about it. *I obviously still do if it's at inappropriate times.* But that's beside the point. I thought something was very wrong with me most of my life. I wished so badly that I'd grow out of these laughing fits that hit me out of nowhere or hit me in the exact moments that I *should not* be laughing. I wanted God to remove it like it was some sort of thorn in my side.

But as life got heavier,

As rumors spread,

As life got turned upside down,

When seasons turned darker than anything I've ever walked through, I realized something: *Laughter really is the best medicine.*

Not because it fixes anything, but because it reminds you that you're still very much alive. I wholeheartedly believe that God wired me this way for a reason. So even in seasons when life got really dark and really heavy, I could still—in some strange and unexpected way—laugh.

Laughing at the Days to Come

There have been seasons, like when I wanted to move to Alaska, that weren't very funny at all. As a matter of fact, nothing felt funny in the least. My joy was depleted, and my hope was running thin. And yet, somehow, I still had slivers of that awkward unexpected laughter. I can remember sitting on my counselor's couch on some of my absolute darkest days. The tears were steady, and the grief was like a heavy brick that had been placed on my chest that made it hard to breathe. And yet, somehow, laughter still managed to find me. That's when I realized how healing it was. A few times the tears would turn into laughter. I was smack dab in the middle of deep, gut-wrenching painful moments, and laughter slipped out of my mouth like it was trying to escape that depressing place deep in my chest. We'd both go from crying together to laughing together in a matter of seconds. It was a confusing phenomenon.

How could laughter and sorrow live in the same room?

The same moments?

The same circumstances?

But I believe, like a lot of things in life, sometimes we overcomplicate it.

Maybe laughter is just proof that grief doesn't win.

It's true what the Bible states in Proverbs 31, "She laughs at the days to come." How could I possibly find anything funny when life doesn't feel funny?

Because laughter is like that.

Well maybe not for normal people.

But it has been at times for me and maybe you too.

It's sneaky.

It surprises you.

Not because life is funny.

Not because you're unbothered.

Not because you're not scared.

But because you know who is ultimately in control. Sometimes laughter becomes a battle cry. It's a way of declaring victory and finding slivers of joy even in our darkest or most awkward moments. Sometimes it's the only sane response when your life feels completely out of control. Sometimes it is God's way of saying: "You're still here."

It's His intimate reminder that you're still breathing.

That your story is far from over, sister.

It's a weapon against the enemy's schemes to steal our joy.

The longer I've walked with Jesus, the more I know this to be true. Joy isn't a feeling; it's a choice. Joy is a Fruit of the Spirit—not a personality trait.

Have you ever blown up balloons for your child's birthday and over-filled any? Sometimes they get so full of air and pressure that you can't even tie them. So you have to release some of it. Laughter kind of is like the same thing for us. When life gets to be too much—full of pressure, pain, and overwhelm—laughter can be a release for *all of that.*

Laughter has a way of sneaking in, just like a young child squeezing their way in the middle of the bed in the wee hours of the night. It sneaks into the moments that may not feel funny, but feel heavy instead. It's God's way of reminding us that the hard times aren't the whole story and there truly is joy in every day in every season. We just have to have an open heart to see it.

And if you're wondering if I only laugh at the worst, most inconvenient or inappropriate times, let me introduce you to a time when motherhood was especially chaotic. On one particular morning, nothing seemed funny, but laughter found its way there. Especially now, looking back.

You may already know this at this point in the book, but I'm kind of a mess. I kind of always have been. I'm scattered as last year's Easter eggs, which are oddly enough, somehow in a basket in my living room in December. I just discovered them this morning. I think I maybe, possibly, at some point, had intentions of creating some sort of game out of them for homeschooling. But like a lot of my ideas, I just didn't see it through. When it comes to structure in my parenting at many times, I have dropped the ball. Maybe it's because I found myself in survival mode for a lot of years.

When I was writing and preparing for this chapter, I went back and read an old blog post I wrote back in September of 2017. At that time in my life, I was twenty-eight and had five kids. My oldest twins were seven, my middle child was three, and my youngest twins had just turned two. I look back on pictures now and laugh so hard that I cry. I didn't know it then, but those hard years were also the best years. In that season, I was struggling. I constantly felt overwhelmed and each day I felt like I was in some sort of video game unlocking a whole new level of survival mode. Because not only was I trying to survive, I was trying to keep all five very small children alive as well. You see, to feral toddlers, everything was a weapon and there were no limits. At least at my house, there wasn't. Not because I didn't try, but because I was outnumbered. If there was a couch or any type of taller surface (like the kitchen counters) they would jump off of it. They made it their goal to test the limits of physics, courage, and my salvation. If there was a tree, they climbed it. And you'd better keep ladders far away from them. And hammers? Death sentence.

Do y'all remember that Miley Cyrus song, "Wrecking Ball"? That was our anthem. My crew came in like a wrecking ball and everyone knew when we had arrived. Someone was always sticky, missing a shoe, possibly naked at times, all with pacifiers hanging out of their mouths. But no worries, because my youngest, most adventurous son often wore a random bicycle helmet on their many adventures (with a mohawk attached to the top for an added flair). It makes me proud to know he was putting safety first in his most adventurous days of being a miniature stunt man. I was also outnumbered, and everyone knew it, especially the kids.

I laugh now looking back, but I didn't always laugh in the moment.

One specific day that year was especially chaotic. It ended in the sheriff, the fire department, the realtor, and Aunt Betty all showing up in my driveway like it was a community open house to my own personal chaos.

It was already a very stressful day, and I heard sirens. We live out in the country, surrounded by cow pastures and not a red light within a few miles of us. So anytime there are a lot of sirens, it signals us to see what's going on in the neighborhood. Most of the time it was by calling my mom, checking the scanner, or stepping outside to see if I could evaluate how far in the distance they were. Shortly after stepping out on the porch, I realized they were all pulling into *my driveway.* The one that had graffiti all down the blacktop from sidewalk chalk and toys scattered like confetti. I'll never forget seeing the fire trucks whip it into my drive. The one with faded Cozy Coupes and bikes piled all the way down, along with bubble wands, little dump trucks, and the scooter with a missing handle. They had no option but to pull through the yard. They dodged the toys without taking out one thing which was quite impressive at the speed they were going. Aunt Betty from down the road also whipped it in right behind them when she saw all the excitement. I was stuck in a state of confusion as to what was happening around me. I know we talked about fight or flight mode in a previous chapter, but have y'all ever found yourself in freeze mode? Where your brain can't quite catch up to the chaos going on around you? So you just freeze, do nothing, no reaction.

That was me a lot of days. Then and now. But especially on that day.

Is there a fire? Is my house on fire? Oh no, where are my kids? They have been quiet for 7.2 seconds, so now that I think of it, that's concerning.

Before I could even think of one more anxious thought, I heard more sirens. And yep, you guessed it, they also arrived in a panic to my humble abode.

Long story short, we were having issues with our alarm system, and there happened to be an on-call feature that would simultaneously signal a panic button. This handy feature would not only call our local police department, but it would also call the local fire department. My wild boys were drawn to all the buttons and took notice anytime they saw me turning it on or off. So, when the emergency personnel explained what had happened, and how they received a call from the panic feature I knew exactly how it went down.

As I was trying to explain to the sheriff what I think may have happened, Dax came outside. Per his regular morning routine to pee off the porch without hesitation (with no clothing might I add). To my horror and shock, he splashed the sheriff's shoes with his urine. That was a moment that I certainly wanted to crawl in a hole and hide for days. A new level of embarrassment was unlocked. Thank God the sheriff was a dad to boys, and he laughed when I could not.

This specific day comes in a close tie with the lovely day that my boys drenched our sweet Schwan's man with the water hose.

That season was one for the books, one that kept me laughing but even more now that I can look back on it.

It was chaos.

Messy.

Unpredictable.

Unfiltered and unhinged.

But still sacred in its own special way.

Perspective Shift

Sometimes we have tunnel vision and can only see what's right in front of us all the many, never-ending messes.

The dishes.

The sippy cups.

The laundry.

Forts everywhere you look.

The parts of our life that aren't quite Instagram worthy.

But when we shift our perspective—even slightly—we start to notice all of the joy threaded into all the chaos. The belly laughs. All of the funny memories that will last forever. Sometimes, it is easier to shift perspective in the seasons where the house is messy and the kids are crazy. It's a little harder when it comes to the tougher things like a diagnosis, a divorce, or a betrayal of some kind. Those are all harder pills to swallow and a little harder to find purpose and perspective in.

It is very possible to still find joy in the spilled Cheerios but more difficult to find it in the spilled hope, spilled dreams, or spilled trust. Those are the moments we have to dig a little deeper until we find the foundation that our joy should be rooted in. The solid foundation of Christ.

This is a time when I want to reiterate something vital that I told you at the very start of this book: Joy and sorrow *can* co-exist. Laughter *can* accompany grief. Peace can shake hands with chaos. Some of life's greatest moments entangle all of these emotions. These emotions aren't the contradiction of one another. They are the evidence of the goodness of God.

So please hear me out, sister. I hope you know at this point in the book that I'm authentic. I am not asking you to fake it til you make it. I'm not about that way of life, not even in the slightest. I would be a complete fraud if I ever tried to tell you otherwise. I'm simply asking that you might consider *noticing* joy where it shows up. Even in small amounts.

In church yesterday, the pastor gave a really good illustration of this and I want to share it with you now. Put down this book for just about ten seconds and look around the room you're in. Look for the color brown and see how many things in your room are brown.

Now, did you notice how many things were red? Probably not. Because the purpose of our perspective was to seek out the things that were brown, right?

How often do we do that in life? I know I do. Some days before my feet even hit the floor, I've determined the mood for the day. When my kids are fighting, when the dishes are piled up, and when nothing seems to be going right. Maybe on the nights I stayed up way too late scrolling on TikTok, looking up conspiracy theories. Or worrying about things I have zero control over. But when we shift our perspective and choose to look for joy, I promise we will find it. Maybe nothing feels funny right now. Just go look at your messy bun in the mirror (I wish I could show you mine right now—I promise you would laugh). In all seriousness, my point is that there is joy and there is laughter in the little things. Sometimes we just don't see it because we are focused on our mess, on our problems, on our depression, on our heartache, on everything else.

Because let's be real for a minute, sis. Sometimes it's hard to find joy and laughter in certain seasons. The news can be super depressing. Our jobs can drain us so much until we feel depleted. The challenges of life and our laundry piles can leave us feeling incredibly discouraged. I get it. Something else I want you to know is this: I'm not talking about faking it until you make it. I'm not about that kind of life. My ministry and my motherhood are built on transparency, authenticity, and surrendering to a perfect God. Because I know I can do nothing apart from Him. He knows our hearts, He knows our struggles in every season. But He offers to carry our burdens for us so that we can rest and find peace. God did not place you on this earth just for you to wash dishes and fold clothes and do it all again the next day. Yes, that may be a large part of our everyday lives. But sometimes we get so caught up in the tasks, that we forget to enjoy the life God has given us. Or sometimes we find our heads barely bobbling for air, because we feel like we are drowning in waters of grief, depression, or overwhelm.

Finding Your Spark Again

One day a few years ago, through tears and a cracked voice, I painfully admitted that my spark was gone. I had gotten caught up that day looking through old pictures and videos of myself mostly before heartache and mostly before walking into a deep depression. That girl seemed like a stranger. That light in her eyes had left in the middle of the night and ran off to another country (or maybe Alaska?).

Sometimes it can be caused by:

- Burnout
- Relationship change
- Trauma
- Depression
- Heartbreak
- Chronic sickness

The best way to find your light again is by looking for the spark. You know the one. That spark that brings you excitement. That thing that is hard to put into words. That spark that makes you feel alive and completely, unapologetically yourself in the best way. It's a certain kind of confidence that has nothing to do with appearance but everything to do with your soul. It's that spark that makes you want to dance in the kitchen to your favorite song. It's the excitement over little simple stuff like your favorite cup of coffee or a conversation with a friend. But sometimes, life has a cruel way of blowing our candles out abruptly. Like a kid at a birthday party that rudely passes by and blows it out before the birthday song is even over. But when we go through seasons where we lose it, we must fight to find it again. Here are a few ways we might find a glimpse of that flicker that once burned brightly:

1. **Seek the Spirit, Not Dopamine:** Turn off your phone. Our culture has tried to convince us that we were meant for constant connection. Constant access 100% of the time to anyone. That, my friend, is a lie. Uninstall Instagram for a week. Try to break the habit of doomscrolling—by the way, this is me preaching to no one but myself over here in my leopard pajamas. Turn off all

the noise and let your brain be quiet. A spark is hard to find in constant noise.

2. **Be Nostalgic:** Think back on things you used to love as a young girl or a young adult and do one of those things. Whether it was a visit to a favorite ice cream place or a hobby like riding a bike. You may just see that it brings you slivers of joy in this season too.

3. **Serve or Volunteer:** This alone has a way of shifting our focus off of the way we feel and helps us have eyes to see others and serve them. When we do that, joy has a way of sneaking back in.

4. **Prayer/Worship Music:** Girl, I cannot tell you how many times this has helped pull me out of a funk. It also confuses the enemy. In moments where we should be on the floor crying and mad at the world, we are praying and praising God for all He is gonna do. Worship has a way of shifting the atmosphere around you for the good!

Here's the thing about a spark: Oftentimes it will go out on its own if it isn't nurtured and protected. Think about when you light a match. Oftentimes, the wind is enough to put it out if you don't guard it with your hand. A spark is a sign of life and hope. It's necessary to ignite. But it cannot sustain and continue burning on its own. Instead, we need a flame.

This is exactly what Scripture means when it says, "Fan into flame for the gift of God" in 2 Timothy 1:6. A spark is that first flicker of hope, God breathing life back into you. But a flame is what happens when you protect and fuel what He is reigniting deep within your soul. Not by trying harder, not by doing more, but by staying closer to the source. Now I know what you're thinking, "You just told me to look for my lost spark, and now you're telling me I need a flame?" No, sister, I'm just telling you what you need to keep that fire going. And I don't mean *you* keeping it going either. Listen, the last time that I was in charge of a bonfire, I nearly burned our house down. So, I'm in no position to lecture you on fire safety. I'm just telling you this—sparks need protecting and flames need fuel. *But not that kind of fuel; please, please don't go start a fire and add gasoline. We're talking about spiritual fires not physical ones.*

The thing is, when we stop trying to keep it burning all on our own and stay connected to our source, it will not burn out. It doesn't mean there won't be days it's a little dimmer, it just means that as long as we stay connected to Jesus, that fire will burn continuously. Because our joy and our happiness aren't found in our circumstances; they're placed in Christ alone.

Proverbs 17:22 says, "A joyful heart is good medicine, but a crushed spirit dries up the bones." Joy matters. It matters because it refuses to let darkness, doom, or dire situations determine our whole story. It matters because it cultivates gratitude. It has a way of shifting our focus off our situation and highlights blessings all around us. Even a giggle can reveal a glimmer of hope, of joy. And like Scripture tells us, it can be the best medicine not because everything is sunshine and rainbows, but because God is good in spite of everything.

You don't have to fake joy. I'm not asking you to slap on a smile and fake it til you make it. I'm just telling you not to feel an ounce of guilt if laughter slips out in the unexpected place like it did for me a few times on the couch in my counselor's office as I was in one of the darkest places in my life. Sometimes it's just coping. It's survival. It's proof that grief doesn't have the final say in our story. It's proof that the enemy's plans against you failed because your joy is rooted in something he can never take away from you: your relationship with God.

So, if any of that sounds familiar, I have a word for you, sister: Your light will return. It won't be this way forever. It *will* come back. Maybe not today, maybe not tomorrow, but I promise you it will. You'll find yourself laughing again, maybe even at the most unexpected or inconvenient times. You'll look in the mirror and see a familiar smile that you haven't seen in a while and you'll know God is still working.

Joy and Sorrow

A gentle breeze from the gulf rustled through the blonde curls of my three-year-old daughter's hair, as she watched her daddy read Mark 2:22, "And no one pours new wine into old wineskins. Otherwise, the wine will burst the skins, and both the wine and the wineskins will be ruined. No, they pour new wine into new wineskins." We stood together next to the ocean; our toes covered in sand as the sun cast a bright orange sky behind us. Our six beautiful children were our audience as we exchanged fresh, renewed wedding vows to one another. It was May of 2023. We were coming out of a very difficult season, after fifteen years of marriage. With the boys in their linen and the girls in their flowy dresses, their sun-kissed cheeks brimmed with joy as they listened intently to every promise we made to one another. I knew the verse their daddy used was likely impossible for their young minds to comprehend.

As their mother, I made a conscious decision to demonstrate the power of that parable through the way I lived my life. For me, that meant moving forward. It meant exchanging heartache and bitterness for grace and forgiveness. I have come to realize that the choice I made, would be a pivotal part of our story. I'm incredibly grateful, that in spite of the storms we weathered, God gave us a beautiful testimony of redemption.

The most difficult seasons, often produce the sweetest fruit. I love how Jesus used the wineskin parable. Old wineskins are no longer elastic. Therefore, they cannot hold the new wine without ruining them and busting the skins. That same stretching God is desiring from us requires obedience. Faith is best demonstrated by fully surrendering our ways, our plans, and our comfort zones. Even if that means walking blindly into unfamiliar territory.

The enemy unleashes any weapon he can to keep us from fulfilling God's ultimate purpose for our lives. Maybe it's the fear that keeps us paralyzed or maybe the pain from the past. But God wants us to leave all of those things behind so that we can fully walk in freedom. If we put too much focus on where we've been, it could hinder where we are going.

Whether it be a friendship ending, a career change, starting over in a new place, or reconciling your marriage, we can absolutely cling to the promise that God is already there.

When struggling with self-worth, we can have complete confidence in Christ.

When we are entangled with fear or anxiety, God will be our refuge.

When the ability to trust is lost, we can wholeheartedly trust in Him.

We cannot fully embrace and receive the blessings God has in store for us if we keep a tight grip on the very things we should lay down at His feet. Only He can bring beauty from ashes. Let us die to the old so that we can be made new. It is then that God will pour out fresh wine in every part of our lives.

In the months prior, I had found myself caught in the fragile crosshairs of a dooming divorce sentence or a fight for my marriage that I didn't even know if I had had the strength for. This generation teaches us that when something is broken you throw it away. But nothing is ever too far gone for God to revive and breathe new life into. Lazarus was dead for three days. The aroma of death lingered around his tomb, but Jesus showed up and *everything* changed.

It was in that season, that a testimony was birthed. One that only God can get the credit for. It didn't happen overnight. It took months of counseling that turned into years. It took many nights of prayers from us and those closest to us that walked through the storms alongside us.

When we surrendered it all to Him, all the brokenness, all the pain, all the heartache, all the regret, all the shame, He began to breathe new life into our lungs again.

Cody and I found our breath again. Together.

Even enough breath to laugh at the days to come.

May joy rise in you again—even in the middle of the mess. May you become the woman who can laugh at the future because we know who is already there, holding it all together for our good and giving us enough grace to giggle along the way.

I want to close this chapter out in prayer.

Dear Lord,

I come to You today with a grateful heart. Thank you for all you are doing in and through this book. I thank you for my sweet sister in Christ who is reading this right now. God, I ask that You meet her right where she is right now. Lord, help her find her spark again, help her joy find its way back into her heart and soul. Life can be cruel, and times can be hard, but we know that You are right there with us in every season. Breathe life into dry bones and help them to come alive stronger and more vibrant than ever before. We know Your word says, "Joy comes in the morning," so help morning to break through the darkness today for my sister. We know You are working and shifting even as we pray. We know that You will restore the spark and fuel the flame like only You can. Thank you, Jesus. In Your precious name we pray,

Amen.

SEPTEMBER 2023 – WE LOVE OUR LITTLE HOMESCHOOL LIFE!

PART 3

God Sustains the Good Work He Starts in You

So many times,
Jesus calls us to
things that are

ANYTHING BUT

COMFORTABLE.

Purpose Where You're Planted

I walked into one of my favorite stores and the first thing I saw was the back-to-school aisle. The cute, colorful banners, the fresh new school supplies, and the cutest matching backpacks and lunchboxes. I got a lump in my throat and fought back tears.

Later that day, I found myself scrolling social media and my feed was flooded with posts all at the same time: "First Day of School!" Lots of cute highlight reels and little outfits and images of my friends' children walking into school for the first time. Mine would have been doing the same thing that day, just like they always had; however, I peered into the back of my twelve-passenger van and my youngest four were with me instead. Earlier in the summer, after a lot of prayer and discussion as a family, my husband and I made the decision to homeschool. I'd spent years dreaming about it, but I always found myself avoiding the leap. I was afraid that I'd not only fall, but I'd nosedive completely and that my poor children would be taking that tumble along with me.

But 2023 was our year! Because I knew God was calling me to it and He had been for years. But there was one issue: I was afraid. I wanted to pick up my phone and make a long-distance phone call to God. It would have gone something like this:

Hey God, it's me, Andi. But you obviously already know that, because You're God. So, I know You want me to homeschool but here is the thing. You know me, You really know me. God, You know I'm a mess. A big mess. I struggle with focus, and I most certainly struggle with fractions. I don't know if I can give them what they deserve, Lord. They're so wise, and smart, and I really feel like they deserve a better teacher than me.

But instead, I called my mom.

By the time I dialed her number, my shaky voice couldn't contain my emotions. I was hoping that she could help me to make sense of that sick feeling in the pit of my stomach. When I heard her gentle voice on the other end of the line, I began to cry. On that specific day, I didn't quite understand those emotions. Because here's the thing, I was so excited for our new adventure! I was ready! I had ordered all of our new curriculum, spent hours researching and planning and it was almost our time to start! But as I saw all of those first day pictures, I felt like I was grieving the familiar life that we'd always known. I was so afraid that I would *fail them*. That fear that crippled me that day, almost made me pull the plug on my faith.

You see, I had complete faith in each of my sweet children. They loved to learn and each of them were so smart in different ways. I fully believed in them but had little to no faith in myself. I always seemed to be my own worst critic, it's something that I still struggle with to this day. So many "what ifs" clouded my judgment.

- What if I wasn't smart enough to do this?
- What if I am the worst teacher on the planet?
- What if I completely fail and end up sending them back next week?
- What if they miss out on the things all of their friends were doing?
- What if I'm not patient enough for this?

I never doubted that this was what God had called me to do, but I didn't really understand *why* He had that kind of faith in my abilities. It was through that, that I allowed the enemy to instill a real fear in my heart that temporarily stole my joy. That very fear created a fog that wouldn't allow me to see past those negative self doubts and all of those "what ifs". I couldn't yet see the beauty that was going to come from our obedience. A mother is usually a good voice of reason. The phone call with my mom helped to remind me of my "why." She helped me to see past all of those negative fears that fogged my vision and helped to replace them with the truths that I knew all along.

That God's grace is sufficient.

That He who called me to it, will absolutely see me through it.

That greater is He that is in me, than He who is in the world.

God's Grace is Sufficient

So many times, Jesus calls us to do things that are *anything but comfortable*. He may call us to things that we feel completely unequipped to do. Just like me as a homeschool mom. I once heard an amazing inspirational message that I sometimes play over and over in my mind. It said: "When God calls you to something, He has already considered who you are."

You see, we don't have to tell God who we are; He already knows. We forget sometimes that He created us in His image, not in the image we think works best for us. He knows our flaws. He knows our weaknesses. He knows our messes. He knows. He knows every single intricate detail about our lives. The good, the bad, and the messy, and all the in between. And when He calls us to something, He doesn't call us based on our abilities. He calls us based on our faith and our obedience.

Sometimes, He asks us to step out of the boat, and simply follow Him. In those moments, we have to keep our eyes on Him. If we focus our eyes on the fog of fear, we just might sink. But if we keep our eyes locked on Him, we will see the blessings on the other side. I have learned through life, and especially throughout my homeschool journey, that when God calls us to things bigger than ourselves, it is then that His glory is on display the brightest.

2 Corinthians 12:9 says, "But he said to me, 'My grace is sufficient for you, for my power is made perfect in weakness.' Therefore, I will boast all the more gladly about my weaknesses, so that Christ's power may rest on me."

Fast forward three years later, and we are still homeschooling. It turns out I most definitely was right about one thing. I'm *not* the perfect homeschool teacher. But perfection is boring anyways, and God never asked that from me. He just wanted me to say "yes" to this journey and trust Him fully and completely. And I am so thankful that I did. My children have thrived at home. We spend our mornings taking our time and they can learn in their own ways, at their own pace, all while being able to learn more about Jesus each and every day. You already know our days are messy. They're filled with a lot of art projects, baking, games, reading, lesson plans, and field trips. Then there is also skating through the house, forts made out of blankets and stacked up textbooks, and don't forget wrestling matches too.

It's safe to say that we are all still learning and growing every day. I've even had to relearn long division. But looking back, I can't imagine if I would have let my fear win and talk me out of this blessing I get to live out every single day.

It was through that leap of faith that God started revealing something vital to me: purpose isn't just what you do, it's what you decide to stay planted in. But friend, this isn't just about homeschool; it's about any place in our lives that God is asking us to be planted even if it's in a place we don't necessarily feel equipped in.

Maybe it's a new career—it's exciting but scary at the same time.

Maybe you're going back to school. Although you're an adult, you made a brave leap to finally do what God is asking of you even when you feel like you may need to brush up on your math skills too.

Maybe you're being called to a new church. This is hard because you are the new girl. You don't know many people yet, but God is still calling you to be planted there in the unfamiliar territory. He's wanting you to lean into the new community, the new ways, but you also find yourself missing your friends at your previous one.

Maybe God is calling you to be a stay-at-home mom, and as much as you want to, you are scared you won't be able to make ends meet.

Or maybe it's a little deeper. Maybe it's your marriage; it's hit rock bottom and you are struggling to find even a sliver of hope. But God asks you to stay even though you don't see any way through the mess your marriage has become.

If this is you, here is what God wants you to know, friend: *Being planted does not mean being punished.* It means God is doing something in you below the surface, something that you can't see just yet. He's growing roots that may feel uncomfortable, but those very roots are producing big faith.

One Step at a Time

One of my very favorite Scriptures comes from the book of Isaiah. Isaiah 43:18-19 says, "Forget the former things; do not dwell on the past. See, I am doing a new thing! Now it springs up; do you not perceive it? I am making a way in the wilderness and streams in the wasteland."

So many times, I have been so guilty of focusing on the former things that it has been hard to see the new things that God is doing. The Word tells us time after time that He will make a way always. He will provide; He is already there. Sometimes God gets our feet moving before we know all the details.

If you're in a season where God is calling you to something new and you're feeling stretched and stressed out, hang tight. Allow me to give you a clearer picture of something I already knew in my bones. Not long after God showed me the promises of stepping into homeschooling, He repeated His message to me in a completely different way. This time the imagery was breathtakingly beautiful under a canopy of live oak trees.

Last spring, I was a chaperone on a trip with my kids to an amazing 4-H camp in *Jekyll* Island, Georgia. That week, our days were filled with adventure. The kids dissected sharks, did saltwater fishing, toured salt marshes, had beach campfires, and so much more. But my favorite part of the trip was something simpler. It was the day we hiked through the maritime forest they had on site. The luscious green plants lined the most gorgeous live oaks I've ever seen. Something about those trees was so majestic. The tour guide talked about how important these trees were to the ecosystem and to that area. Their roots all grew out of the ground horizontally and lined the pathways throughout the forest. Their massive and widespread root system was like nothing I'd ever seen before. I couldn't stop looking at those roots, and no one around me seemed as intrigued as I was.

Standing there, underneath the lush canopy of Spanish moss, standing on the roots that intertwined all around it, I knew God was speaking to me. The structure and resilience of the live oaks reminded me of women, moms, and wives when they are rooted in Christ.

I know He was already planting this very chapter of this book that I hadn't even begun writing yet deep in my heart. He was showing me, in real time, the meaning of *purpose where you're planted*. You see, those trees had stood tall for so many years. They'd withstood many storms and hurricanes. But they didn't survive hurricanes because they were pretty and majestic. They survived because they were rooted. It doesn't mean those storms didn't come, but their roots made them resilient.

Here's something else about those roots. Your girl did some digging (see what I did there). I wanted to know *how* those exquisite trees lived hundreds of years. I learned in my research that live oaks are among the oldest living trees in North America. Their deep widespread roots anchor them firmly into the ground, which makes them a lot less likely to topple over when winds come their way.

It all goes back to the roots. There is something incredibly special about the root system of a live oak; it's called root interconnectivity. Their roots can intertwine with neighboring trees, which creates a strong system that also acts as a powerful defense when storms do come. You see, those roots and their intention and purpose is very similar to God's plans for us. Think of it like locking arms with someone in a windstorm. Together, our strengths help to stabilize one another. God rarely grows purpose in isolation; sometimes He calls us to a place of isolation to grow with Him and to pray, but He won't leave us there.

He often grows purpose through connection. Connection to Him first through walking with Him daily. And He strengthens our roots with community. Sometimes that's through small groups, a new fellow homeschool mom, or through friendships that He plants next to us in the season we will need it most. Through your friend who you know you can always call to pray over you and your situation. Those connected roots help anchor you and keep you from standing alone.

Have you ever considered that God has strategically placed you exactly where you are in this season or at this place or in this environment for a purpose? A divine purpose that may be difficult to see just yet. And you know what else? Sometimes it may not even be *for you*. It may be for the person you work with in the cubicle next to yours who is struggling silently with their faith and is in a deep depression. They may need to see the love of Jesus desperately. And God sent you. Yes *you*. He chose you to be the one to help pull them out of the pits.

Consider that for a minute, friend.

You may not see how you can even be used by God, because you struggle with the confidence to even share your testimony. But He's already doing it. Without you realizing it. Just by you showing up. By you staying planted. You see your flaws, but He sees your faithfulness. And your calling has nothing at all to do with your confidence, friend, instead it's about the One who called you.

And that marriage that looks hopeless, the one that God told you to stay in, what if you are just a few prayers away from a breakthrough? In a world that tells people to run as soon as it gets hard, stay. Trust God's timing; He is never late, but always on time. So, when you stay planted and rooted and still, it gives Him the space to resurrect that love that used to flood your home.

Rooted in Jesus

I know our stories are not all the same and solutions are not always a "one size fits all." But when we stay planted and rooted in Christ, He can create strong roots that will withstand any storm. I want to encourage you to grow roots where you're planted. And if that's a struggle, start small with something like this. Start with one small step or "root" a day:

1. **A daily anchor in the Word.** Even if it's one verse. Write it on your heart daily, sister. Live it out. Repeat it to yourself until you can say it with confidence.

2. **One honest prayer.** This may look similar to the call I wanted to place with God about me homeschooling. It's ok to bring it all to Him. It looks like saying, *"Lord, I'm scared." "Lord, please help me stay planted when I really wanna run back to my comfort zone." "Lord, give me a little extra grace to get through the day."* Simple prayers create big impact. Honest prayers grow deep roots in our relationship with Christ.

3. **Stay connected; don't isolate.** Hear me out, I have a major tendency to do this. I once heard, "you know who your true friends are they are the ones who check on you when you go a little quiet." That's fitting for me. Maybe it's fitting for you too. Because when I get stressed and overwhelmed, I tend to check out and leave texts on read. Text one safe person who you can trust. Join the small group. God often strengthens us through

people. Remember that those interconnected roots bind together against any winds that life blows our way.

4. **Stay planted long enough to see the fruit.** So many times,
    when we are out in uncomfortable or unfamiliar territory, we
    will bail before we see the breakthrough. Some of God's best
    work happens beneath the surface. It may take a while to see
    impact or the fruit. In the meantime, be still and wait it out.

God will plant us to withstand whatever storm we may face. Just like
those trees have those root structures in their DNA, so do we, because
Jesus' blood runs through our veins. We just have to stay rooted.

Live oaks are a true testament to endurance. But they didn't become
resilient overnight. Roots take time. The same goes for us in wherever
God plants us. When you stay rooted to God and intertwine with the
right Christian people, your branches may bend but you won't break.
Here's the thing, friend. If you are struggling with stepping out in faith
in any situation just know that you aren't alone. If you find yourself in a
similar situation, cling to this truth: God doesn't call the equipped, He
equips the called. Have peace in knowing that His grace will meet you
every step of the way.

If you would have told me that day in that back-to-school aisle, the
day I had a mini meltdown, that God was about to make this the sweetest
part of our story, I probably would have laughed, cried, and called my
mom again. But here we are on the other side of His promises still struggling a little with long division but so thankful for how our roots have
grown and spread in this season. And I, Andi Harper, am proof that God
doesn't need a perfect teacher for my babies, He just needs a willing one.
And I can tell you firsthand that when He plants you somewhere new, He
doesn't leave you to fend for yourself or to figure it out alone. He supplies
plenty of grace to get you through each day. And thank God, His mercies
are new each morning.

I wish I could tell you that now that I'm on the other side of that specific season that I am fearless. But that would be a lie. The difference now

is this—I've seen the goodness of God too many times to believe the fog anymore. So now I trust without hesitation. Knowing He will never leave you or forsake you. But He will stretch you a little along the way. Because oftentimes those very places are where our purpose is planted.

THE LIVE OAK TREES IN JEKYLL ISLAND, GEORGIA WITH PAISLEE AND DAX

Your calling doesn't show up when you're **FULLY DRESSED, CAFFEINATED, PREPARED, AND READY TO SERVE.** *It shows up when you're tapped out, overwhelmed, and hiding in your bathtub."*

Your Calling Isn't Cancelled by Your Chaos

Sometimes, in the middle of your ordinary chaos, God sends you a Korean son out of nowhere.

Early in the spring of this year, my son was celebrating his birthday with a few friends. I was introduced to his newest friend, a foreign exchange student from South Korea. He was so excited to be invited to Hudson's birthday bonfire, a small gathering we had planned with his closest friends. He burned his hand while making a s'more and he frantically ran to me to help him. He gave me the craziest look when I put mustard on his burn. If you're from the South, your grandma probably taught you a whole list of tricks to get you through life. Tips and tricks for a bad cold, a colicky baby, a bee sting, or a burn. To his surprise and slight disgust, the bright yellow condiment smeared on his hand did the trick and it helped draw the burn out. From then on out, he started to call me Mustard Lady, and we all got a good laugh out of it.

As weeks went on, Hyung started to come to our home more often and also began attending church services with us. If we had family dinners, he would tag along. Every holiday, cookout, or any random adventure, Hyung came along. During the summer, he also got to attend church camp with my older kids at the beach, where he was baptized.

Effortlessly, Hyung became part of our family. He may have looked a little different from us, and talked a little different from us, but he was just like one of my own. Before long, I found myself tripping over his shoes and breaking up friendly games of wrestling that he was always right in the middle of. You see, to many people, wrestling may look like a sign of division or quarrel but in our house, it is a sign of love and adoration. I tell people all the time that wrestling is a love language in our home. Although Hyung was with us a lot, we weren't his host family. Until one night when that all changed.

But first, I have a confession to make, I used to smoke occasionally when I got really stressed out. I'm not proud of it, but it was a stress reliever. My boys are all really wild and they break things. Lots of things. In the past couple of months, they have ripped cabinets off the hinges by accident. They've also gone tumbling into the walls and dented up the drywall.

So now, even though I don't smoke, I do have another stress outlet. Scalding hot baths. That's my "me time." Think a sauna and a hot tub mixed together and there you'll find me.

Boiling myself like a frog, in a sad attempt to relieve my stress and worries from the day.

One night, I was soaking in my hot bath when my son began banging on the door to my bathroom. I could tell he was very upset about something from the urgency in his voice.

"Mom, Hyung is on the phone, he is crying, he is being removed from his host home. He's gonna have to move to another town for the rest of his time here. And mom, he asked if we would take him."

A million thoughts raced through my mind. We would have to find an extra bed; we were maxed out. We'd most certainly have to buy extra food, because we all know how growing teenage boys eat. Then there were the extra forms; I had heard the application process was a nightmare. I was already strapped for time. Could I really take on another kid right now? I was writing a book after all and managing lots of messes and schedules and homeschool and all the other duties that go along with our crazy life.

I already knew we loved him. A lot. That wasn't a question. But my question was: would he really love us if he lived with us 24/7? I mean, in our house, the chaos doesn't stop; you get a front row seat at any given time, all the time.

Before I could drum up any more fears or questions, I felt a nudging from the Holy Spirit, and my heart answered before my brain could catch up.

"Yes."

Because you see, love trumps all those other worries and fears. That love was enough for me to say yes, in spite of my fears. In spite of my worries. In spite of anything else. Because I knew, deep in my heart that God was calling us to this.

The next few days after that were a bit of a blur. We had to prepare for a home inspection, fill out hours' worth of paperwork and prepare our hearts for the outcome either way.

There was no guarantee that we would be approved and there was also a chance that Hyung would be sent to another town, another school, and another family. And that alone, broke our hearts and made us hit our knees in prayer.

By Friday of that week, we did the home visit and got the stamp of approval. We signed papers and were officially Hyung's legal guardians. In a matter of a few days, our family of six kids turned to seven kids as Hyung became ours. (Side note: If my kids happen to read that line this would be the section when they would yell sixxxx-sevvennnnnn. Now carry on.)

With each day that passed after that it became harder to remember our lives before Hyung. He was the puzzle piece that was missing in our big, crazy family. Here's a nugget of truth I want you to grab hold of, sister: *Your calling isn't cancelled by the chaos; it's revealed in it.*

The Perfect Time to Say Yes to God

There's a good chance that your chaos doesn't look just like mine. You may not have six kids or a bonus Korean son, but you have your own kind of crazy too. We all do. Maybe you're a taxi for your kids and their lengthy list of extracurricular activities. They're living their best lives and you're their ride. Or maybe you spend your days wrangling a feral toddler. You baby proof everything, but they unlock a new danger like a stunt man every time their feet hit the floor. Perhaps you're navigating the teenage years. You're doing all you can to be a loving parent but everything you say is "cringe," and they discover new ways to be frustrated with you daily. Whatever it is, whatever your season, you don't have to wait for life to be calm to say "yes" to the call.

Sometimes your calling doesn't show up when you're fully dressed, caffeinated, prepared, and ready to serve. It shows up when you're tapped out, overwhelmed, and hiding out in your bathtub. Do you ever find yourself putting things off like this:

"I'll do it when we have a bigger house."

"I'll say yes when I make more money."

"I'll do it when things settle down."

That was me too, sister. Over the years, I have talked myself out of so many things because of the busy life we lead. But if you've ever believed the lies that your calling has to wait until life slows down, I'm here to gently tell you that it *never will*. Yes, there are slower seasons, but there will never be a perfect time to say "yes" to God. But it's important that we do it anyway.

So, ask yourself what does this calling look like for you in your life, practically?

And your calling may not be hosting an exchange student. Instead, it may be saying "yes" to a mission trip you've eyed for years. Or waking up extra early on Sundays, instead of sleeping in so that you can serve in kids ministry. It may be starting a small group, even with your packed schedule, so that you can create connection and discipleship with other women. Maybe it's finally taking a leap of faith and launching a new business you've dreamed of for years. The calling can look like saying yes in small, ordinary ways, without waiting for the perfect moment or ideal setup. It looks like obeying that nudge from God even when you feel overwhelmed and underqualified. Right smack dab in the middle of your sticky floors, messy van, and a schedule that feels more like a circus. If God brings you to it, He will see you through it.

Something vital that the Bible demonstrates to us is that Jesus made time for interruptions. Some of His greatest miracles took place in those interruptions. God created each of our babies on purpose, but He also made them ours on purpose. And I fully believe He created Hyung just for us too. God didn't just send Hyung into a calm, quiet, perfect household. He sent him into ours—which was quite the opposite. It's loud, messy, and a tad bit dysfunctional. And once Hyung made himself at home, he didn't just get our best moments he got our real ones too. He also wasn't exempt from the sibling arguments. In fact, our boy Hyung was a bit of a tattle tale. It was quite hilarious. This trait came in handy after school. They would all race to the van in mad dash, backpacks flying, arms flailing, all in an attempt to snag the front seat. Once they fought it out, Hyung would buckle up and immediately give me a full report of his day. But before he told me about his own day, he had to report to me all about Paislee having too much screen time at school. Then, he'd next report on his brother, Hudson who he saw goofing off in the hallway. Shortly after, he would most definitely tell on his younger siblings for aggravating him. I would do my best to hold back the laughter, but it was hard to contain some days. But if that's not family, I don't know what is. Not the absence of chaos, but Hyung thriving smack dab in the middle of it.

Not only was he not exempt from sibling scuffles, Hyung also wasn't exempt from loading the dishwasher. He learned to pitch in too, and he did it well. Even on days like the rest of the kids had when they needed a reminder. He even cooked for us. Amazing, authentic Korean dishes. Hyung didn't just learn about us, we learned so much about him and his culture.

When it came to our time with Hyung, we didn't put things off. It had a way of shifting our perspective. We knew his time with us wasn't forever. His departure date couldn't be ignored. It was loud and stood out in our minds a date we all dreaded so badly. But we didn't postpone joy because of it. We took the spontaneous trips. Lots of them. We tried the new restaurants. We made time in our schedules for board games and charades and movie nights. We made the memories. In fact, we made more memories over several months than many people do in years. Because we knew we had a timeline.

I cried when reflecting back on this. It convicted me, but in the best way, of just how often I delay things that matter most because I'm waiting on life to slow down. But when you have limited time, it shifts your perspective. Because you know that you don't have forever. And when you know you don't have forever, you stop saying, "I'll do it later," and replace it with, "I'll make the time because this matters." And that is the vital part about answering the call on your life. Being willing to say yes even when the timing seems less than perfect. Choosing not to delay obedience opened up the door to an opportunity to see some of God's biggest blessings in life.

The one thing that connected us all was our faith. We had the best, real, authentic conversations about Jesus. About our faith, our beliefs, and our convictions. We also had some tough conversations about morals and making good choices. The previous host home that Hyung was in wasn't a Christian household. And first and foremost, God knew he needed that. While he was with us, we witnessed his faith grow and a spark ignite for the Lord. And now, while back in South Korea, he attends Bible study weekly.

We laughed together and cried together, and we also gave lots of hugs. Hyung was the first kid each night to say, "Goodnight, love you," to every member of the family. And it makes my heart gleam with pride to tell you that he still does this each night over texts or video calls.

He didn't need a perfectly put-together home; he needed one with love. And he gave that love right back. He needed one that had Jesus in the center of it. And one that fully realized that blood doesn't make a family . . . love does. And that's the part I want you to lean into, friend. Hyung didn't join us because we were prepared or because we were ready. He was brought to us because God knew our hearts were prepared. God trusted us with him in our real, authentic, messy, chaos. And I don't even want to think about what we would have missed if we had said no to that nudge.

One crowded Sunday morning service at church, Hyung stood next to me during worship. And as the worship team sang, Hyung sang a little louder. That's the thing about Hyung. He loves to sing. And he doesn't care who's listening. Most teenage boys won't worship authentically in the middle of a crowded Sunday service. But Hyung did. With his whole heart, and his whole deep, Korean voice. He didn't care if it was off tune because his focus wasn't on that. It was on his worship. He wholeheartedly loved Jesus out loud. His heart posture was something we could all learn from. And that's when my tears began to fall. And I thought to myself, what if we would have missed this? What if we would have said no to that nudge? I felt an intense wave of gratitude hit me right in my soul. God didn't wait for our lives to slow down before He trusted us with a holy assignment. He dropped it right in the middle of our mess and He met us there with grace and more love than I could ever imagine. This call didn't look like a stage or a microphone. It looked like making room, squeezing in another bed, gathering extra groceries and pulling up another chair at the table. The call looked like growing our family in the most beautiful and unexpected way possible.

For Such a Time as This

As I was writing this, I found an unexpected parallel between this chapter and Esther in the Bible. Esther beautifully displayed the definition of calling showing up at unexpected and inconvenient timing. She too wasn't quite ready in the way we'd imagine. And her assignment came with great risk, much more so than most of our assignments today. The very lives of her people weighed heavily on her shoulders. Esther wasn't just a pretty face. She had courage to be obedient and bold for the Lord. She wasn't born into royalty; she was an orphan who had been kindly raised by her uncle. The king chose her because of her beauty, but I believe she was placed in her position because of the favor of God on her life. He had His favor on her.

Have you ever been there? Been in rooms you can't explain being in? Brushing shoulders with people who you otherwise wouldn't be eating with except that God placed you there. Have you ever had an opportunity that had no explanation but God. God has a way of placing us in positions He knows we will glorify Him in.

You see, when a death sentence hovered over her people, Esther had to stand in between fear and faith. This would have been the moment that I would have wanted to run fast. She didn't wake up one morning with a strategic plan, she was simply placed in position. Strategically. Quietly. Right where God could use her. And when that moment came, she could have fled, stayed silent, or waited for the conditions to be more favorable. But she lived out Mordecai's words and let them echo into the chambers of her soul. Esther 4:14, "And who knows but that you have come to your royal position for such a time as this?"

For such a time as this. That verse is comforting yet convicting. Comforting because it is an epic reminder that God positioned you. But it is convicting because it is a bold reminder that our delay can look like disobedience especially when God is nudging you to move. Esther's calling wasn't based on comfort; it was based on how she handled herself under pressure.

Now I know that your "For such a time as this" doesn't look anything like hers. As for my "for such as time as this" moment, it wasn't in a palace, it was in my bathroom that I was hiding out in. Mine didn't come from a crown it came from a phone call. It came from rearranging our lives a little so that God could show us what was missing all along.

And sister, your "for such a time as this moment," won't look the same either. It might just look like making room, showing up, and saying yes in the moments where God is nudging you right where you are.

I'm amazed every day at how God works behind the scenes in every intricate detail. I never would have imagined that the exchange student that came to my son's bonfire and had his first s'more would one day have a permanent place in our family and in our hearts. I never knew it was possible to love a child so much that I didn't give birth to. Throughout our journey with him, we found that love transcends bloodlines, distance, and time. It stretches across continents and lasts forever. Hyung has gone back home. Saying goodbye was one of the hardest things all of us have ever had to do. We cried for weeks. I don't know if we loved too hard or if it was because Hyung was too hard not to love so much. But not a day has gone by that we haven't talked since then. We've gotten to talk with his amazing family as well and I'm thankful that they share their amazing son with us. In a way, we are all connected even on opposite sides of the world.

To Hyung, you will always be one of ours. Thank you for letting us love you and thank you for bringing each of us joy and laughter every single day. You made each day an adventure and somehow, you made our chaos even sweeter. Our home is always your home, and you always have a permanent place in our hearts. You'll forever be a seventh child to Cody and me and a sibling to the kids. We love you forever.

So friend, let this be your reminder that if God is nudging you too, say yes. It may not look perfect, but it will be there where you'll discover purpose. Because your calling isn't cancelled by your chaos; it's revealed in it.

Confidence is built

BY TRUSTING THE ONE

who called you.

You Were Built for This

On a tattered page of an old journal beside me contains a beautiful, stained affirmation that I wrote years ago. It is handwritten, a little messy, with an orange magic marker. In the center of the words, held a spill, likely from a sippy cup, causing the words to bleed through. But its message still pierces my soul now as it did when God first spoke it to me.

I remember the season. I even remember the specific day. I found myself looking in the mirror, feeling broken but clinging desperately to the only One that could bring me peace. Surrender looked a little scary, but I knew I could trust God with my life and my future.

The affirmation read like this:

"I know when I don't have confidence in myself, I have confidence in you. I know when I feel not quite good enough that you are more than enough. When I struggle to trust, I will trust you, God."

I wonder how different our lives may be if we started each day with a surrendered heart. If we took a long look in the mirror, unafraid of the brokenness in the reflection staring back at us. If we refused to focus on our lack but instead we saw our abundance in Christ. What if, instead of picking ourselves apart each day, we allowed God to define our reflection? Because, at some point or another, every woman wrestles with confidence and finding the courage to keep showing up anyway.

You Belong Here

Last summer, I found myself in a place that I was a little uncertain of. Though I did all the planning and cleared my schedule, when it came time for the event, I got cold feet. As I pulled into the parking lot, I began to see all different kinds of women walking into the hotel where the event was taking place. I just sat in the car and looked at the messy passenger seat next to me. It held my broken high heel and the dumped contents of my makeup bag. You see, I tried to get ready in the car, because I hate wearing heels, but as soon as I stepped out on the car door, my heel broke. Did I mention that I hate high heels? To top it off, I had been desperately looking for mascara to swipe on my lashes, so that I might feel a tad bit more put together. And in an attempt to find it, everything toppled out and spilled onto the seat of that little Nissan I had borrowed for my drive. I looked in the mirror and loudly proclaimed to myself, "You do not belong here." I didn't feel as put-together as those other women. I don't typically wear business attire. I rock leggings and oversized T-shirts, along with my comfy flip-flops.

Before I could say another word, God checked me real quick.

In my spirit I heard His response to me, "Yes, you do. Now find some other shoes and step out of that car. I sent you there." It was in that moment, when I heard the voice of the Holy Spirit, that I was reminded that confidence has nothing to do with my feelings or my insecurities. It has nothing to do with "looking the part." Confidence is built by trusting the One who called you.

Do you know what the root word of confidence is? Confide. To confide means to trust. You see, we don't have to have confidence in ourselves when we have confidence in Christ. Because He said it, I believe it.

Isaiah 6:8 says, "Then I heard the voice of the Lord saying, 'Whom shall I send? And who will go for us?' And I said, 'Here am I. Send me!'"

So if He sent me there? I'll go. I'll raise my hand and say, "I'll go." I'll walk into that room boldly, maybe even a little wobbly, because I'll even go with a broken high heel if I have to. I'll walk into that room like He sent me there, because I know without hesitation that He did. You see, I don't have to have confidence in myself to have full confidence in the One who sent me.

Rebuilding Your Wall

The Holy Spirit brought the story of Nehemiah to my mind when writing this very last chapter. Nehemiah had an assignment, and he didn't step into it because he felt qualified; he stepped into it because he knew God called him. I'm sure he felt a little intimidated. I know I would have.

The book of Nehemiah is a beautiful illustration of not only the physical rebuilding of a wall, but also the spiritual rebuilding that took place while restoring the people of Jerusalem. The assignment God gave Nehemiah felt bigger than him. He had a heavy heart and was burdened for the city of Jerusalem. Nehemiah was the cupbearer of the King. After much prayer, he approached the King and asked if he could go help to rebuild the walls of Jerusalem. Long story short, not only did the king *allow* him to do that, but he sent an army with him. That's what I call provision. That's the beautiful character of God.

Nehemiah never panicked. When opposition came, and trust me it did, he combatted the enemy's tactics with righteousness, wisdom, and perseverance. He prayed continuously. He would rally the army with words of encouragement and had them pray as well. When the warfare kept coming, his hands never stopped. He would continue building with one hand, holding a sword with the other one.

Nehemiah's enemies showed up continuously throughout the building process. They were loud. They mocked him. They ridiculed him. They made plots to bring him harm. They incited fear and created distractions. They tried every way possible to abort the mission that God had sent him to complete. Scripture tells us that Nehemiah was unphased and stayed strong in the Lord. He kept his eyes on the mission, in spite of all the warfare.

What if we all came together despite our flaws and failures for one purpose? And we began building together in unity? Look at what we could accomplish for the Kingdom.

God worked through Nehemiah and the wall was built. It was completed. Because Nehemiah never stopped in spite of the obstacles and attacks of the enemy. History tells us that others attempted and failed for seventy-two years. But when God sent Nehemiah it only took fifty-two days.

Nehemiah 6:3 says, *"I am doing a great work and I cannot come down."* What a convicting scripture for me to reflect on. When I read that verse, I asked myself this:

- How often have I come down from the wall because the enemy intimidated me?
- How many times have I allowed fear to have the final say?
- How many times have I stopped in my tracks because I listened the lies instead of leaning into God's truths?

What wall have you come down from because you struggled with confidence? Or trust?

No, we aren't building city walls, but we're building homes. We're building ministries. We're building healthy marriages with God in the center. We're building families built on Christian values.

Philippians 1:6 says, *"Being confident of this, that he who began a good work in you will carry it on to completion."* Your wall will be completed. God will see it through. I can't tell you how many tears I have cried the past few weeks as I am *finally* seeing this book come to completion. This book was my own wall. It was an assignment and a dream

God gave me so many years ago. But many times, life got messy, and I lost my way a little. I came down off my wall. I allowed the enemy to distract me and to delay me, but God never allowed him to destroy me.

And during that time, God never once looked at me in frustration. He never said, "Forget it, she's never gonna come around" or "I'll find someone else because she will never be healed enough." He never once cancelled my assignment no matter how long it took me to start building again. Instead, He met me in the delay, in the heartache, in the mess, and did His own building within me until I came back to it.

The older I get, the more I realize that the goal isn't to look the part—it's to be with Jesus. To be so near to Him that His character rubs off on me and pours out into every area of my life. That the overflow of His grace spreads into my marriage, my children, my ministry.

Recently I was reading in the book of Acts and a verse stood out from the pages. Acts 4:13 says, "When they saw the courage of Peter and John and realized they were unschooled, ordinary men, they were astonished and took note that these men had been with Jesus." And that's when I realized that's all I want. For people to see the life I live and also think to themselves, "She's been with Jesus."

NOT "She's been with Tiktok."

NOT "She's been with the world."

NOT "She's been with the crowds."

Not any of that, just Jesus.

The disciples didn't have fancy degrees.

They didn't have it all figured out.

They had just been with Jesus.

That's all I want. And I know that's all you want too.

Sister, I want to encourage you not to come off your wall. Keep building, even if it takes ten years, twenty years. Just don't stop. Keep building. One prayer at a time. One surrendered morning at a time. One "yes" at a time, even in the face of uncertainty.

You are anointed and appointed for this assignment, sister.

God placed you as the mother of those babies because He trusts you with them.

God called you to that business because you are going to use it for His glory.

God called you to that marriage because He is using your faith to grow your husband closer to God. And together, the impact of that unity in Christ will shake generations to come.

You were built for this not because you have endless amounts of energy and patience, but because God is with you. You were built for those babies you care for each day. You were built for this life because I know who built you. I know the builder. And when He created you, I imagine how He must have felt after His creation was complete. He saw you and called you His masterpiece. He looked upon your face and saw His handiwork, His likeness, and His reflection. And this is really what my whole book has been based on. Never once did God call us to be perfect, polished, or have it all figured out, but He did create each of us with a purpose.

And friend, if this book did anything, I pray it helped you to realize that you aren't in this alone. I hope that my messy, funny stories echo through your heart as a permission to finally breathe again. In a world of pressures and highlight reels, I hope you can rest in knowing that God never expected perfection out of you. He's always spoken to me in the unlikely places. I've heard His voice clearly at the sink full of dishes, while in a car with a broken high heel, and in seasons with a broken heart. Through delayed dreams and prayers written in random notebooks. That stained page with the words written with an orange magic marker wasn't ruined. It was proof that I'm still here. Proof that even when we spill coffee on our plans, His promises remain the same. It was a promise that He will see me through it all; the messy, the mundane, and the uncertain.

So if you close the pages and all you can see is your mess; Jesus doesn't mind.

He just wants you to be with Him. Messy bun, messy house, and all.

Because there is mercy in the messes.

There is calling in the chaos.

And there is plenty of grace that covers all the rest.

And sister, I hope you choose purpose over perfection every single day.

THANKSGIVING 2025 – OUR BIG, HAPPY, RAMBUNCTIOUS FAMILY.

Acknowledgements

First and foremost, I owe my greatest thanks to our Heavenly Father. Without the work of the Holy Spirit, this book never would have been written. God has shown me the power of Romans 8:28 faithfully, all throughout my life.

Cody—Thank you for being my biggest cheerleader in every big dream that I have, especially this one. From juggling the kids and extra jobs so that I could write and get this book published…your love and sacrifices have never gone unnoticed. I'm incredibly grateful for the way that you love me and our kids. There is no one else I'd rather live this crazy, beautiful life with. I love you forever.

Paislee—Thank you for being my sidekick in all things ministry and thank you for reminding me of how far I've come in my journey. You can always talk me into a coffee date and you never fail to stop and notice the ones who need love the most. Your tender heart and ambition in life makes me so incredibly proud every day. I love you more than words.

Cozi—Thank you for never minding my mess, even when it may drive you crazy at times. You help keep our chaos in order and you are the biggest help to me. Your drive, determination, and big heart will take you so far in life. Your grit and spitfire personality make you, *you*. But your love for Jesus is my favorite. I love you so much.

Tillie—Thank you for being my biggest hype girl and keeping my heart young. You never fail to tell me that I'm "the best mommy ever," even on the days I feel like I'm failing. Your sass and personality keep me on my toes. No matter how big you get, you'll always be momma's baby. I love you forever.

Hudson—Your ability to find beauty in the smallest things is one of my favorite traits about you. I know I can count on you for honesty and a laugh. I love your kind heart and I'm so incredibly proud of you. No one quite knows the depths of your giving heart, and it makes me so proud. I love how you love your momma and always protect me fiercely. I love you so much.

Dax—You have such a gift for connecting with people. Your kindness and ability to love others so well is a true inspiration to me. Thank you for meeting me with so much grace, even when I haven't cooked sloppy joes as often as you'd like while writing this book. You have a calling on your life and I cannot wait to see what comes from it. I love you to the moon.

Cub—I wish I could see life through your eyes sometimes. Your imagination and love for adventure makes raising you so magical. You may test my patience and my sanity…but you always make me laugh harder than anyone. Every single day is fun with you, my sweet, rambunctious boy. You are just as big hearted as you are full of energy and I'm so thankful you are mine! I love you so much.

Hyung—You will forever be our seventh child. Thank you for showing us pure, unconditional love that knows no limits, no matter how many miles are between us. Thank you for never failing to message us daily when we are apart, and for still keeping us on our toes. We couldn't love you any more if you were our own blood.

Mom and Dad—Thank you for supporting all of my dreams and for praying for me always. There were many days that I never would have made it through without your unconditional love and guidance. Thank you for raising me with bold convictions and strong morals that have carried me where I am today. I love you more than words could say.

Nana—Our trip for me to finish my manuscript will always be one of my favorite memories. Thank you for always making everything so special. I know that no matter where life takes me, you are always in my corner. I love you so much.

Hannah—Thank you for never hesitating to drop all of your plans to help me in any way with the kids or to pick me up a coffee during this book writing process. You love so selflessly and that's what makes you so special. You'll always be my ride or die. Love you so big.

Rhonda and Rusty—Thank you for feeding our big family multiple times a week throughout this book process, without any complaints. But let's be honest, you did that before the book. I'm incredibly thankful to have such great in-laws. Love you all so much.

To my family and friends—Your encouragement to me has helped push me to the finish line. From encouraging texts, days of praying fiercely over me, and simply reading chapters and providing feedback-none of it goes unnoticed. Thank you from the bottom of my heart.

To the one who purchased my very first copy, my sweet Chloe—I love you so much. You reminded me year after year that one day I'd be selling my own books at conferences. Thank you, sister.

To my incredible team of editors—This book wouldn't be so beautifully put together without all of your help and hard work. You are incredibly talented, wise, and kind. I'm grateful for each part that you all have played to help me make my dreams come true! You helped this first time author feel heard, valued, and encouraged.

About the Author

Andi Harper is a Christian author, speaker, and podcast host who is passionate about encouraging women in every season of life. Through her honest storytelling, humor, and biblical truth, she reminds women that God can bring beauty even in the messes.

She is the Christian hype girl you never knew that you needed.

As a busy mom, she spends most days in the beautiful chaos of motherhood- homeschooling, cheering from the sidelines at her kids' sporting events, and losing the keys to her twelve-passenger van more often than she cares to admit. She also loves traveling, hiking, and random taco dates with her husband.

Andi lives with her family in Kentucky.

Let's Connect

www.andiharper.com

Facebook: Andi Harper
Instagram: @Andiharper_
Tiktok: @AndiHarperOfficial
Email: andi@andiharper.com

To book speaking engagements:
Email andi@andiharper.com

Want more encouragement?
Join my email community for a free resource.
Scan QR code below!

One last thing . . .
If this book encouraged you,
Leave a review
Tag me on social media
Share it with a friend